# QUICKBOOKS PRO DESKTOP USER GUIDE 2024

### A Step-by-Step Handbook for Efficient Bookkeeping and Finance Management

## MICHEL M. DUNCAN

# TABLE OF CONTENTS

# DISCLAIMER

The contents of this book are provided for informational and entertainment purposes only. The author and publisher make no representations or warranties with respect to the accuracy, applicability, completeness, or suitability of the contents of this book for any purpose.

The information contained within this book is based on the author's personal experiences, research, and opinions, and it is not intended to substitute for professional advice. Readers are encouraged to consult appropriate professionals in the field regarding their individual situations and circumstances.

The author and publisher shall not be liable for any loss, injury, or damage allegedly arising from any information or suggestions contained within this book. Any reliance you place on such information is strictly at your own risk.

Furthermore, the inclusion of any third-party resources, websites, or references does not imply endorsement or responsibility for the content or services provided by these entities.

Readers are encouraged to use their own discretion and judgment in applying any information or recommendations contained within this book to their own lives and situations.

Thank you for reading and understanding this disclaimer

# CHAPTER ONE
# INTRODUCTION

## Overview of QuickBooks Pro Desktop

QuickBooks Pro Desktop is a financial accounting software program designed for small and medium-sized businesses. It offers a wide range of features to help businesses track their income and expenses, manage inventory, create invoices and bills, and generate financial reports.

Here's a closer look at some of its key functionalities:

- **Streamlined Invoicing and Sales Management:** QuickBooks Pro Desktop allows you to create professional invoices, track sales receipts, and stay on top of who owes you money.

- **Efficient Inventory Management:** The software helps you manage your inventory levels, track product costs, and generate inventory reports.

- **Simplified Bill Management:** Easily manage your bills and track accounts payable to ensure timely payments to vendors.

- **Enhanced Financial Reporting:** Generate insightful financial reports such as profit and loss statements, balance sheets, and general ledger reports to gain a deeper understanding of your business performance.

- **Bank Reconciliation:** Reconcile your bank statements quickly and efficiently to ensure your accounts are accurate.

## Target Audience

QuickBooks Pro Desktop is ideal for small to medium-sized businesses across various industries, including retail, manufacturing, professional services, and non-profits. It caters to business owners, accountants, bookkeepers, and financial managers who need a reliable and comprehensive tool for managing their finances.

Whether you are new to QuickBooks or transitioning from another accounting system, QuickBooks Pro Desktop offers a powerful solution to streamline your financial operations and help your business thrive.

QuickBooks Pro Desktop is an on-premise accounting software, meaning the data is stored locally on your computer. This can offer some advantages in terms of security and data privacy for some businesses. However, it also means that you'll need to back up your data regularly and ensure your software is up-to-date.

QuickBooks Pro Desktop is a powerful and user-friendly accounting solution for small and medium-sized businesses. If you're looking for an on-premise accounting software with a wide range of features, then QuickBooks Pro Desktop could be a great option for you.

## System Requirements

The system requirements for QuickBooks Pro Desktop will vary slightly depending on the year of the version you plan to use. Here's a breakdown of the requirements for the most recent version, QuickBooks Pro Desktop 2024:

**Operating System:**

- Windows 11 (64-bit) or Windows 10 (64-bit) versions supported by Microsoft.

**Processor:**

- Minimum: 2.4 GHz processor

**Memory (RAM):**

- Minimum: 8 GB of RAM
- Recommended: 16 GB of RAM

**Hard Drive Space:**

- Minimum: 2.5 GB of free disk space (additional space required for data files)
- Recommended: Store your QuickBooks data file on a solid-state drive (SSD) for optimal performance.

## Additional Requirements:

- Internet connection (for product registration, downloads, and some features)

- Microsoft .NET 4.8 Runtime (provided with the installation files)

**Important Note:** These are the minimum system requirements. If you plan to use advanced features or have multiple users accessing the software simultaneously, you may need a more powerful computer. It's always best to check the latest system requirements for your specific version of QuickBooks Pro Desktop before purchasing or installing it.

## Installing QuickBooks Pro Desktop

These instructions are general and may vary slightly depending on your specific version of QuickBooks Pro Desktop.

## General Installation Steps:

1. **Download the QuickBooks Pro Desktop installation file:** You'll need to download the installation file from the Intuit website. You'll typically find this download link within your Intuit account after purchasing the software.

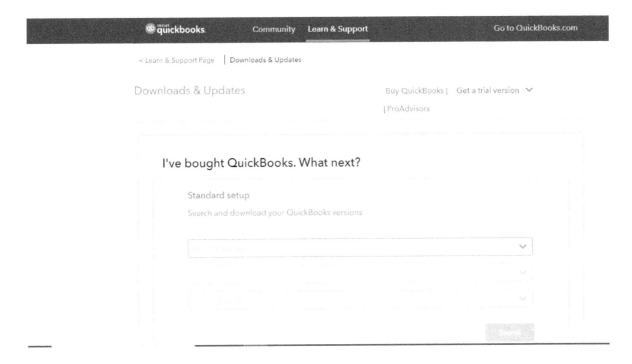

Here's your product

Select your product
1   Already have a license? Select the version you want to download   —

QuickBooks Desktop Pro 2021

**Download**

Version: 2021 (United Kingdom) 32-bit | Size: 668 MB

Already Downloaded?  Get the latest updates
Release: Release 4(R4) | Size: 97.8 MB
What's New?

Not what you were looking for?  Search again

2. Double-click the downloaded installation file: This will launch the installation wizard.

3. Follow the on-screen instructions: The installation wizard will guide you through the steps required to install QuickBooks Pro Desktop on your computer. This will typically involve accepting the license agreement, selecting an installation location, and choosing components to install.

4. Enter your license key (if prompted): During installation, you may be prompted to enter your license key. Have your license key readily available before starting the installation process.

5. Complete the installation: Once you've followed the on-screen instructions, the installation process will be complete.

6. Launch QuickBooks Pro Desktop: You should now be able to launch QuickBooks Pro Desktop from your Start menu or desktop shortcut.

If you encounter any issues during installation, consult the Intuit QuickBooks documentation or support resources for troubleshooting assistance.

## Getting Started with QuickBooks Pro Desktop

Getting started with QuickBooks Pro Desktop involves setting up your company file and familiarizing yourself with the basic functionalities. Here's a breakdown of the initial steps:

1. **Create a New Company File:** When you launch QuickBooks Pro Desktop for the first time, you'll be prompted to create a new company file. This file will store all your financial data for your business.

2. **Set Up Your Company Information:** Input your business name, address, contact information, and fiscal year-end date.

3. **Customize Your Chart of Accounts:** The chart of accounts is a list of all the income and expense accounts used in your business. QuickBooks Pro Desktop provides a default chart of accounts, but you can customize it to fit your specific needs.

4. **Add Customers and Vendors:** Enter information about your customers and vendors, including their names, addresses, contact information, and payment terms.

5. **Set Up Inventory (if applicable):** If you manage inventory, you'll need to set up your inventory items, including product names, descriptions, quantities, and costs.

6. **Connect Your Bank Accounts (Optional):** QuickBooks Pro Desktop allows you to connect your bank accounts for easier reconciliation and automatic downloads of transactions.

7. **Explore the Interface:** Take some time to explore the QuickBooks Pro Desktop interface and familiarize yourself with the menus, buttons, and features.

Remember, this is a general overview of getting started. The specific steps may vary depending on your business needs and the version of QuickBooks Pro Desktop you're using.

# CHAPTER TWO
# SETTING UP YOUR COMPANY FILE

## Creating a New Company File

Ready to get started with QuickBooks Desktop? Let's set up your company file with your own business information!

1. **Open QuickBooks Desktop:** Double-click the QuickBooks icon on your desktop or find it in your Start menu.

2. **Create a New Company:** You'll see a window asking if you want to open an existing company or create a new one. Choose **Create a new company**.

3. **Quick Start or Deep Dive?** QuickBooks offers two options:

   - **Express Start:** Perfect if you're eager to jump in. Just provide your business name, industry, and type. You can fill in more details later.

   - **Detailed Start:** This option lets you enter all your company info right away for a more complete setup from the beginning.

4. **Fill in Your Business Details:** No matter which setup method you pick, you'll need some basic information:

   - **Business Name:** Your official business name.

   - **Industry:** Choose the category that best fits your business type.

   - **Business Type:** Are you a sole proprietor, partnership, corporation, etc.?

   - **Fiscal Year End:** The date your fiscal year ends (used for annual reports).

5. **Customize Your Accounts (Optional):** QuickBooks comes with a pre-made list of accounts for income and expenses (called the chart of accounts). You can review and adjust these accounts to better match your specific business needs. You can do this now or later.

6. **Finalize and Go!** After entering your company info and making any adjustments to the chart of accounts, follow the on-screen instructions to complete the setup. QuickBooks will create your new company file, and you'll be ready to manage your finances!

## Bonus Tips:

- Don't worry, you can always edit your company info or accounts later.
- QuickBooks offers a sample company file as a reference while setting up your own.
- Take advantage of the resources and tutorials from Intuit to get the most out of QuickBooks Desktop!

## Customizing Your Company Settings

QuickBooks Desktop offers a variety of settings you can customize to fit your specific business needs. Here's a breakdown of how to access and navigate these settings:

## 1. Accessing Company Settings:

- Open QuickBooks Desktop and ensure you have your company file open.
- Go to the **Edit** menu located on the top menu bar.
- Select **Preferences** and then choose **Company Preferences**.

## 2. Navigating Company Preferences:

Within the Company Preferences window, you'll find several sections for customizing various aspects of your company file. Here are some of the key sections:

- **Company Information:** Edit your business name, address, contact information, and fiscal year end date.
- **Charts of Accounts:** Manage your chart of accounts, which includes adding, editing, or deleting accounts used to categorize your income and expenses.
- **Taxes:** Set up your sales tax codes, payroll taxes, and other tax-related preferences.
- **Invoices & Statements:** Customize the look and feel of your invoices, sales receipts, and statements sent to customers.

- **Other Preferences:** This section includes various additional settings such as company logo, fonts, and defaults for different functionalities within QuickBooks Desktop.

## 3. Making Changes and Saving:

- Once you're within a specific section (e.g., Company Information), you can find editable fields and options to customize the settings according to your preferences.
- After making your changes, be sure to click **Save** to apply them to your company file.

**Important Note:** While QuickBooks Desktop allows for customization of various settings, it's important to consult with a qualified accountant or tax advisor for guidance on specific tax-related settings or configurations.

By following these steps and exploring the different sections within Company Preferences, you can tailor QuickBooks Desktop to streamline your financial management processes and ensure your data is categorized and organized according to your business needs.

# Setting Up Users and Permission

QuickBooks Desktop allows you to grant access to your company file to multiple users. This can be beneficial if you have employees who need to help manage your finances.

However, it's important to control what each user can see and do within the software to ensure data security and accuracy. Here's a breakdown of how to set up users and permissions in QuickBooks Desktop:

## 1. Accessing User Management:

- Open QuickBooks Desktop and ensure your company file is open.
- Go to the **Company** menu located on the top menu bar.
- Select **Users and Roles**.

## 2. User Roles vs. Individual Users:

- QuickBooks Desktop utilizes a permission-based system controlled through **roles**. Each role defines a specific set of permissions for users assigned to it.
- You can create **custom roles** tailored to your needs, or you can use the **predefined roles** provided by QuickBooks Desktop (e.g., Admin, Accounts Payable, Sales).

### 3. Creating a New Custom Role (Optional):

- In the **Users and Roles** window, select the **Role List** tab.
- Click **New** to create a new custom role.
- Enter a descriptive name for the role and choose a permission level (Full Access, Edit, View).
- Navigate through the different sections (e.g., Customers, Vendors, Banking) and set specific permissions for each area. You can choose **None**, **Full**, or **Partial** access for each section.
- Once you've defined the permissions for all sections, click **OK** to save the custom role.

### 4. Creating a New User:

- In the **Users and Roles** window, select the **User List** tab.
- Click **New** to create a new user.
- Enter a username and password for the new user.
- From the **Available Roles** list, select the appropriate role (predefined or custom) that defines the user's permissions within QuickBooks Desktop.
- You can also enter the user's email address for potential password reset functionalities.
- Click **OK** to save the new user.

### 5. Managing Existing Users and Roles:

- The **Users and Roles** window allows you to view, edit, or delete existing users and roles.
- You can assign different roles to existing users or modify the permissions within a custom role.

## Additional Considerations:

- It's recommended to create unique usernames and passwords for each user to maintain accountability.
- Assigning the least privilege principle is recommended. Grant users only the permissions they need to perform their specific tasks within QuickBooks Desktop.
- Regularly review and update user permissions as your business needs evolve.
- By following these steps, you can effectively set up users and permissions in QuickBooks Desktop, ensuring your financial data is secure and accessible to authorized users with the appropriate level of access.

# Importing Data from Other Software

QuickBooks Desktop doesn't support directly importing data from other software through functionalities like Python code. However, it offers alternative methods to bring your data into QuickBooks Desktop:

- **Manual Entry:** While not ideal for large datasets, you can manually enter your data into the appropriate fields within QuickBooks Desktop. This might involve entering customer information, invoices, or expenses directly into their designated sections.
- **CSV or Excel Import:** QuickBooks Desktop allows you to import specific data sets from CSV or Excel files. It's important to format your data following specific guidelines to ensure a smooth import process.

*Here's a general overview of the CSV/Excel import process:*

- **Prepare your data:** Ensure your data in the CSV or Excel file is formatted correctly according to QuickBooks Desktop's specifications.
- **Open the import wizard:** In QuickBooks Desktop, navigate to the menu option for importing data (specific location may vary depending on the version).
- **Select the data type:** Choose the type of data you're importing, such as customers, vendors, or invoices.
- **Browse for your file:** Select the CSV or Excel file containing your data.
- **Map your data:** Match the fields in your file to the corresponding fields in QuickBooks Desktop. QuickBooks will try to automatically map some fields, but you may need to manually review and adjust the mapping.
- **Import your data:** Once you've confirmed the mapping, initiate the import process. QuickBooks Desktop will import your data into the designated sections of your company file.

**Important Note:** It's recommended to consult QuickBooks Desktop's documentation or support resources for detailed instructions and troubleshooting steps specific to the data type you're importing. By understanding these methods, you can choose the approach that best suits your needs for importing data into QuickBooks Desktop.

# CHAPTER THREE
# NAVIGATING QUICKBOOKS PRO DESKTOP

## Understanding the QuickBooks Home Page

The QuickBooks Pro Desktop Home Page is designed to be a central hub, providing an overview of your financial data and offering easy access to frequently used features.

*Here's a breakdown of the key elements you'll find on the Home Page:*

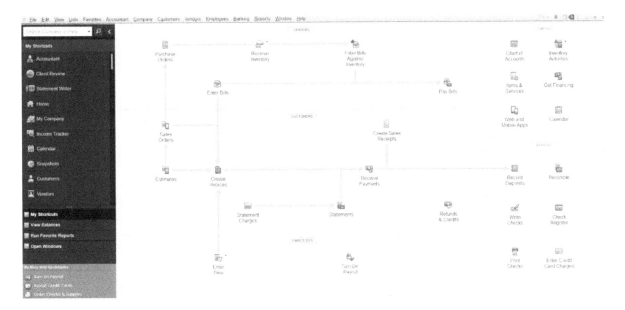

## 1. Company Information:

- This section might display your company name and logo (if uploaded).

## 2. Insights (Optional):

- This section provides a visual overview of your financial health using graphs and charts. It might display metrics like income trends, expenses by category, or accounts receivable aging. (Availability depends on your version of QuickBooks Pro Desktop)

## 3. Activity Centres:

This is the core functionality of the Home Page. It typically displays a grid of icons representing various financial activities categorized by sections like:

- **Customers:** Create invoices, receive payments, manage customer data.
- **Vendors:** Pay bills, enter expenses, track vendor information.

- **Employees:** (if applicable) Manage payroll tasks (limited functionalities in QuickBooks Pro Desktop).
- **Banking:** Reconcile bank statements, manage deposits, write checks.
- **Inventory:** (if applicable) Track inventory levels, manage purchase orders.

### 4. Customization Options:

- You might be able to personalize the Home Page by hiding or rearranging the activity centre icons to prioritize the features you use most frequently. This allows you to tailor the Home Page to your specific workflow.

### 5. Search Bar:

- The Home Page might include a search bar that allows you to search for specific transactions, invoices, or customers within your QuickBooks Pro Desktop file.

## Benefits of Using the Home Page:

- **Centralized Overview:** Provides a quick snapshot of your financial health and key metrics (with Insights).
- **Easy Access:** Offers one-click access to commonly used features for managing customers, vendors, employees, banking, and inventory (if applicable).
- **Customization:** You can personalize the view to prioritize the functionalities most relevant to your day-to-day tasks.

Overall, the QuickBooks Pro Desktop Home Page serves as a valuable starting point for navigating your accounting software and managing your finances efficiently.

## Using the Menu Bar and Icon Bar

QuickBooks Pro Desktop offers two main navigation elements to access features and functionalities: the Menu Bar and the Icon Bar. Here's a breakdown of how to use them effectively:

### Menu Bar:

Located at the top of the QuickBooks Pro Desktop window, the Menu Bar provides access to a comprehensive range of features categorized by logical sections.

***Here are some common menu options:***

- **File:** Used for tasks related to your company file, such as opening, saving, creating backups, or exporting data.

- **Edit:** Offers editing functions for modifying data within your company file.

- **Company:** Manage company information, preferences, and settings.

- **Lists:** Access and manage lists of customers, vendors, employees, accounts, and other essential data elements.

- **Customers:** Navigate to functionalities related to managing customer data, creating invoices, recording sales receipts, and processing customer payments.

- **Vendors:** Access features for managing vendor information, entering bills, tracking expenses, and paying bills.

- **Employees:** (if applicable) Manage payroll tasks and employee information (functionalities might be limited in QuickBooks Pro Desktop).

- **Banking:** Reconcile bank statements, manage deposits, write checks, and categorize banking transactions.

- **Reports:** Generate various financial reports to analyse your business performance, income, expenses, and other financial metrics.

- **Taxes:** (if applicable) Access functionalities related to managing sales tax, payroll taxes, and other tax-related tasks (might require additional setup).

- **Help:** Provides access to built-in help resources, tutorials, and the option to contact QuickBooks support.

<u>Icon Bar:</u>

The Icon Bar, typically located on the left side of the window (but can be repositioned on top), offers quick access to commonly used features and functions. It displays icons that represent specific tasks or windows within QuickBooks Pro Desktop.

***Here's how to use it:***

- **Clicking an icon:** Opens the corresponding window or function associated with that icon. For example, clicking the "Customers" icon might open the customer list window.
- **Customizing the Icon Bar:** You can personalize the Icon Bar by adding or removing icons to prioritize the features you use most frequently. This customization is typically done through the "View" menu option.

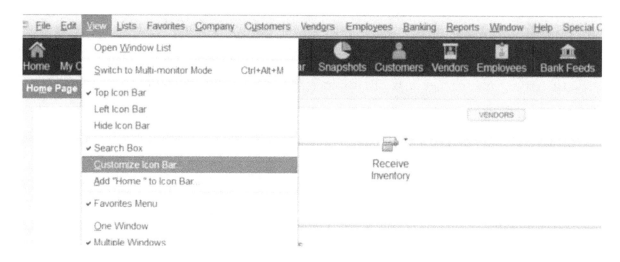

### Using Menu Bar and Icon Bar Together:

The Menu Bar and Icon Bar provide complementary navigation methods. The Menu Bar offers a more comprehensive breakdown of functionalities categorized by logical sections, while the Icon Bar provides quick one-click access to frequently used features.

*Here's a recommendation for efficient navigation:*

- Use the Menu Bar to explore the entire range of features and functionalities offered by QuickBooks Pro Desktop, especially when you're new to the software.
- Once familiar with the software, leverage the Icon Bar to customize it with the features you use most often for a streamlined workflow.

By effectively using both the Menu Bar and Icon Bar, you can navigate QuickBooks Pro Desktop efficiently and access the tools you need to manage your finances effectively.

# Customizing the QuickBooks Interface

If you frequently use specific features in QuickBooks, you can customize the interface to highlight what's most important to you. Here's how:

## Set Up Your Default Workspace

You can configure QuickBooks to automatically display specific transaction windows when you open the program.

1. Open a Transaction Window:
   - Open a frequently used window, such as Write Checks.
2. Save Your Workspace:
   - Go to the **Window** menu.
   - Select **Workspace**, then **Save Workspace**.
   - Repeat these steps for any other transaction windows you frequently use.

The next time you open QuickBooks, these windows will be arranged according to your saved preferences.

## Customize Your QuickBooks Toolbar

Customize the toolbar to streamline your daily tasks.

1. Open Toolbar Settings:
   - Go to the **QuickBooks** menu and select **Settings**.
   - Choose **Toolbar/Tabs**.
2. Modify Toolbar Display:
   - Select **Display Toolbar** to show the toolbar while using QuickBooks.
   - Choose how you want the toolbar to appear: **Vertical** or **Horizontal**.
   - Select **Keep Vertical Toolbar Expanded** to keep it open at all times.
3. Add Icons or Windows to the Toolbar:
   - Drag and drop icons or transaction windows onto the toolbar to add them.
   - Rearrange icons by dragging them within the toolbar.
4. Create Links to Transaction Windows:
   - Open the desired transaction window.

- Select **Customize** on the toolbar.
- Drag the window to the toolbar.
- Add a description and choose an icon for the link.

<u>**Use Tabbed Windows**</u>

Optimize your workspace by using tabbed windows.

1. Open Tab Settings:
   - Go to the **QuickBooks** menu and select **Settings**.
   - Choose **Toolbar/Tabs**.
2. Enable Tabbed Windows:
   - Select Use Tabbed Windows.
   - Organize your windows by:
     - ✓ Tab Similar Windows Together: Combine similar windows (e.g., forms, reports).
     - ✓ Tab All Windows Together: Combine all open windows.

<u>**Use Dark Mode**</u>

For macOS Mojave (10.14) and later, you can enable Dark Mode in QuickBooks.

1. Enable Dark Mode:
- Go to the **Apple** menu and select **System Settings**.
- Choose **General**, then select **Dark**.

Note: QuickBooks will use the accent colour you select for icons and buttons

# <u>Customize the Colour of Your Account Registers</u>
Assign colours to account registers for a personalized touch.

1. Open an Account Register:
- Open any account register.
2. Change the Register Colour:
- Select the colour dropdown at the upper right.
- For more options, select **Other** to open the colour palette.
- Choose the desired colour for the register. The content, text, and rows will appear in this colour.

3. Adjust Text Colour:

- If you don't want the text to match the register colour, uncheck **Allows Colour Text** in the colour dropdown.

By customizing these settings, you can make QuickBooks more intuitive and tailored to your workflow.

# Using QuickBooks Centres

QuickBooks Pro Desktop utilizes a concept called "Centres" to organize and manage essential financial data. These Centres function as dedicated workspaces for specific tasks, allowing you to efficiently manage customers, vendors, employees, and other financial elements.

***Here's a breakdown of how Centres work and how to leverage them effectively:***

## Accessing Centres:

There are two primary ways to access Centres in QuickBooks Pro Desktop:

1. **Home Page:** The Home Page typically displays a grid of icons representing various Centres, such as Customers, Vendors, Employees, and Banking. Clicking on a specific icon will open the corresponding Centre.
2. **Menu Bar:** The Menu Bar also provides access to Centres through dedicated menu options. For instance, clicking the "Customers" menu option will open the Customer Centre.

## Common Centres in QuickBooks Pro Desktop:

- **Customers Centre:** This Centre allows you to manage your customer data, create invoices and sales receipts, record customer payments, and track outstanding balances.
- **Vendors Centre:** Here, you can manage vendor information, enter bills for purchases, categorize expenses, and process payments to vendors.
- **Employees Centre (if applicable):** This Centre is used for managing payroll tasks and employee information (functionalities might be limited in QuickBooks Pro Desktop compared to dedicated payroll software).
- **Banking Centre:** This Centre is where you can reconcile bank statements, manage deposits and checks, categorize banking transactions, and download bank feeds (if enabled).

- **Inventory Centre (if applicable):** This Centre helps you track inventory levels, manage purchase orders, and adjust inventory quantities (availability depends on your version of QuickBooks Pro Desktop).

## Using Centre Features:

Each Centre offers a set of tools and functionalities specific to its purpose. Here are some general actions you can typically perform within a Centre:

- **Create new entries:** For instance, you can create new customer profiles, enter bills from vendors, or add new employees (if applicable).
- **Edit existing data:** Modify information for existing customers, vendors, or employees.
- **Search and filter:** Locate specific entries within a Centre using search bars and filtering options.
- **Generate reports:** Run reports specific to the Centre's data, such as customer balance reports, vendor transaction reports, or payroll summaries (if applicable).

## Benefits of Using Centres:

- **Organized Workspace:** Centres provide a dedicated workspace for managing specific aspects of your finances, promoting a more organized approach.
- **Improved Efficiency:** By keeping related tasks and data centralized within each Centre, you can streamline your workflow and find what you need quickly.
- **Data Segregation:** Centres help segregate customer, vendor, and employee data, making it easier to focus on specific aspects of your finances.

Overall, QuickBooks Pro Desktop's Centres offer a user-friendly way to manage your financial data and perform essential accounting tasks within a categorized structure.

# CHAPTER FOUR
# MANAGING CUSTOMERS AND SALES

## Setting Up Customer Information

As your business grows, it's critical to be organized and maintain track of your consumers. In QuickBooks Online, you may create customer profiles and link them to transactions or invoices. QuickBooks Online allows you to manage your customer base efficiently.

Here's a breakdown of how to add new customers, import them from Excel, create sub-customers, and manage existing customer information. Here's how to add and update your customer list.

### Adding a New Customer:

1. Go to **Sales** and select **Customers**.

2. Click **New customer**.

3. Enter a **Customer display name** (required). This is the name that will appear on invoices and other customer-related documents.

4. Fill out any additional customer information in the provided sections. This might include contact details, billing address, shipping address, and other relevant information.

5. Click **Save** to create the new customer profile.

## Importing Customers from Excel:

If you have a list of customers in an Excel spreadsheet, you can import them directly into QuickBooks Online:

1. Go to **Sales** and select **Customers**.
2. Click the dropdown arrow next to **New customer** and select **Import customers**.
3. Click **Browse** to locate your Excel file and select it.
4. Follow the on-screen steps to map the fields in your Excel sheet to the corresponding fields in QuickBooks Online.
5. Choose the customers you want to import and click **Import**.

## Creating Sub-Customers:

Sub-customers are useful for managing customers who are part of a larger organization or group. Here's how to create a sub-customer:

- Go to **Sales** and select **Customers**.
- Click **New customer**.
- Enter the sub-customer's name and contact information.
- Check the box labelled **Is a sub-customer**. This will display a dropdown menu for selecting the parent customer.
- Select the appropriate parent customer from the dropdown menu.
- Choose whether to bill the sub-customer with the parent customer by checking the **Bill parent customer** box.
- Fill out any additional information for the sub-customer.
- Click **Save** to create the sub-customer profile.

## Managing Existing Customers:

QuickBooks Online allows you to edit, delete, activate/inactivate, and merge customer profiles:

- **Edit Customer:** Go to **Sales** > **Customers**, select the customer, click **Customer Details**, then **Edit** to modify their information.

- **Delete Customer (Make Inactive):** Go to **Sales** > **Customers**, select the customer, click the dropdown arrow next to **Edit**, and choose **Make inactive**. (This hides them from lists but preserves their transaction history).

- **Activate Inactive Customer:** Go to **Sales** > **Customers**, click the **Settings** icon, check the **Include inactive** box, locate the inactive customer, and select **Make active** from the **Action** column.

- **Merge Duplicate Customers:** Ensure both profiles lack sub-customers. Go to **Sales** > **Customers**, open the unwanted profile, click **Edit**, enter the name of the profile you want to keep (ensuring an exact match), click **Save**, and confirm the merge when prompted.

By following these steps, you can effectively manage your customer base in QuickBooks Online, ensuring accurate record-keeping and efficient customer management.

## Creating Estimates and Quotes

QuickBooks Pro Desktop allows you to create professional estimates and quotes to present potential pricing to your clients before converting them into invoices. Here's a step-by-step guide on how to create estimates:

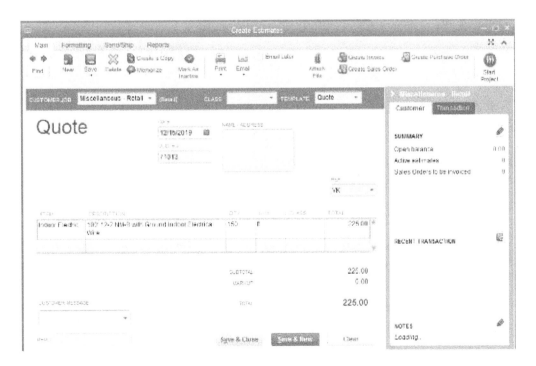

1. Enable Estimates (if necessary):

   - Go to **Edit** menu > **Preferences**.

   - On the left pane, select **Jobs & Estimates**.

   - In the **Company Preferences** tab, ensure "**Do you create estimates?**" is selected as **Yes**.

   - Click **OK** to save the preference.

2. Create a New Estimate:

   - Go to the **Customers** menu and select **Create Estimates**. (Alternatively, you can access it from the **Home** page if the Estimates icon is displayed).

3. . Customer and Job Information:

   - In the Customer: Job dropdown, select the customer you're creating the estimate for. If the customer isn't already in your system, you can add them by selecting Add New.

   - If the estimate is for a specific job, choose the relevant job from the dropdown menu. You can also create a new job by selecting Add New.

   - Estimate Details:

   - Enter the Estimate Date at the top.

   - The Estimate Number will be automatically generated by QuickBooks.

   - You can add a brief Description of the project or service being estimated.

4. Adding Items and Services:

   - In the line item section, you can either:

   - Select existing items or services from your product/service list by clicking the dropdown menu in the Item column.

5. Add a new item or service by clicking the + Add New option. This will allow you to define the details like description, price, and account information for the new item.

   - Enter the Quantity of each item or service being included in the estimate.

   - The Rate (price per unit) will automatically populate if you selected an existing item/service. You can modify the rate if needed.

   - QuickBooks will calculate the Amount (quantity x rate) for each line item.

6. Additional Options:

   - You can add a Discount to the entire estimate by entering a percentage in the Discount field.

- The Total amount of the estimate will automatically update based on the line items and any applied discount.

- You can add a Memo at the bottom to include any additional information for the client.

7. Customizing the Estimate (Optional):

   - Depending on your version of QuickBooks, you might be able to customize the layout of the estimate form. This could involve:

     ✓ Adding your company logo.

     ✓ Modifying fonts and colours.

     ✓ Editing the header and footer information. (Note: Extensive customization might be limited).

8. Saving and Sending the Estimate:

   - Once you've reviewed the estimate details, click Save.

   - QuickBooks will give you options to:

     ✓ Save & Close: Saves the estimate without sending it to the customer.

     ✓ Save & Email: Saves the estimate and opens a new email window with the estimate attached for you to send to your client.

     ✓ Save & Print: Saves the estimate and allows you to print a physical copy.

## Additional Tips:

- You can create estimates for customers without assigning them to a specific job if needed.

- Consider using estimate templates if your estimates tend to follow a similar structure for different projects.

- QuickBooks allows converting estimates into invoices once the client approves the project and you're ready to proceed with the work.

By following these steps, you can create professional and detailed estimates to present to your clients in QuickBooks Pro Desktop. This can help you communicate project pricing effectively and secure client approval before converting the estimate into a billable invoice.

# Invoicing Customers

QuickBooks Online allows you to create professional invoices, manage them efficiently, and ensure timely payments from your customers.

*Here's a guide on creating invoices, customizing them, and managing the invoicing process:*

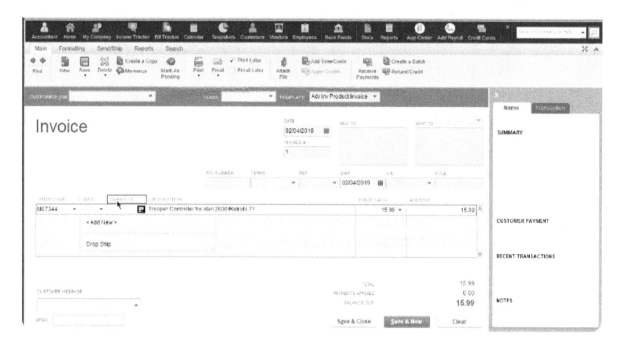

## Creating an Invoice:

1. Go to the + **New** menu and select **Invoice**.

2. From the **Customer** dropdown, choose the customer you're creating the invoice for. If the customer is new, click **Add New** to create their profile.

3. (Optional) Enter a **Due date** for the invoice payment.

4. In the product/service section, you can either:

    • Select existing items from your product/service list.

    • Click + **Add New** to create a new item for the invoice.

5. Enter the **Quantity** of each item or service being invoiced.

6. The **Rate** (price per unit) will populate automatically if you selected an existing product/service. You can modify the rate if needed.

7. QuickBooks will calculate the **Amount** (quantity x rate) for each line item.

8. (Optional) Add a **Sales tax** by selecting the appropriate tax rate from the dropdown menu.

9. (Optional) Add a **Discount** to the entire invoice by entering a percentage in the **Discount** field.

10. The **Total** amount of the invoice will update automatically based on the line items, taxes (if applicable), and any applied discount.

11. You can add a **Memo** at the bottom to include any additional information for the customer.

12. Click **Save** to create the invoice.

## Saving and Sending Options:

- **Save:** Saves the invoice without sending it to the customer.
- **Save & Send:** Saves the invoice and opens a new email window with the invoice attached for you to send to the customer.
- **Save & Print:** Saves the invoice and allows you to print a physical copy.

## Customizing Invoices:

You can customize the look and feel of your invoices by editing the invoice template. This might include:

- Adding your company logo.
- Modifying fonts and colours.
- Editing the header and footer information.

## Managing Invoices:

- You can view a list of all your invoices in the **Sales** menu under **Invoices**.
- The invoice list allows you to search, filter, and sort invoices based on various criteria.
- QuickBooks Online lets you edit existing invoices, mark invoices as paid, send payment reminders, and even create recurring invoices for ongoing services.

# Receiving Payments

When a customer pays you for an open invoice, you must input the payment into QuickBooks. The Accounts Receivable workflow includes the recording of invoices.

On Windows or Mac, enter a sales receipt if your buyer paid in full up front, or a payment item if they just paid a portion of it. If you use Intuit Merchant Services, here's how you can process your customers' credit or debit cards on Windows or Mac.

*Here's a guide on recording customer payments in QuickBooks, covering both Windows and Mac versions:*

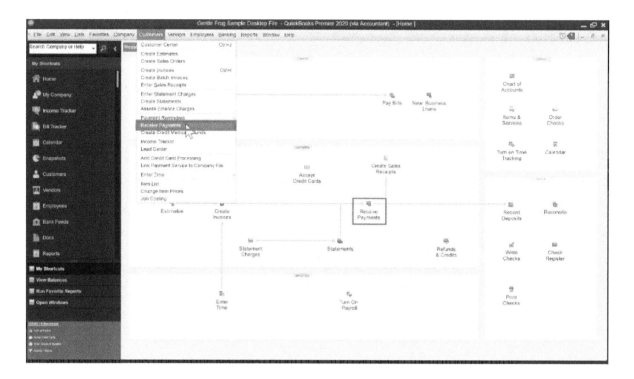

## Process Overview:

1.  Access the Receive Payment Function:

    *   Windows: Go to the Home page or the Customers menu, and select Receive Payment.

    *   Mac: Go to the Customers menu and select Receive Payments or Create a Payment.

2.  **Customer Selection:** Choose the customer's name from the **Received From** dropdown menu (Windows) or the customer list (Mac).

3.  **Payment Details:**

    *   Enter the **Amount received**.

    *   Verify the **Date** is correct.

    *   Select the **Payment method** used (cash, check, etc.).

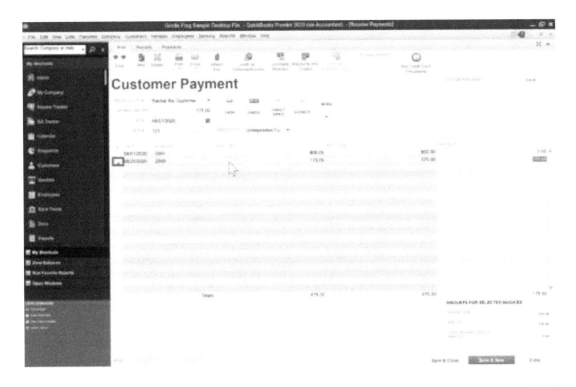

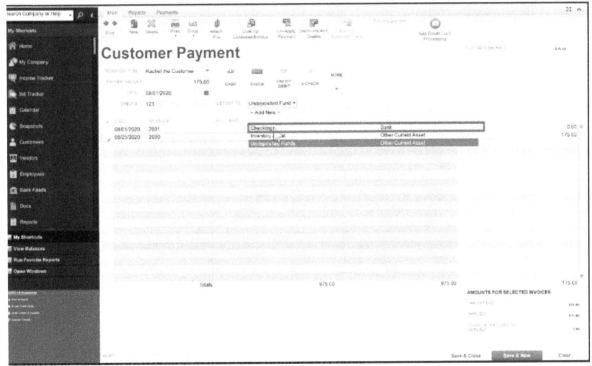

1. **Invoice Selection:** Choose the specific invoice(s) being paid for by checking the corresponding boxes.

2. **Discounts and Credits (Optional):** If applicable, select **Discounts and Credits** to add a discount or credit to the payment.

3. **Saving and Depositing:**
   - **Windows:** By default, payments go to the **Undeposited Funds** account. You can learn more about this account or change the default deposit account.
   - **Mac:** Choose how you want to deposit the payment:
     - ✓ **Group with other undeposited funds:** Holds the payment in the Undeposited Funds account.
     - ✓ **Deposit to:** Specify a specific bank account for the deposit.
1. **Save and Close:** Finalize the process by clicking **Save & Close** (Windows) or **Save** (Mac).

## Additional Notes:

- **Editing Payments:** To modify a recorded payment, simply select it from the list and edit the information.
- **Customer Payment History:** View the payment history for a specific customer by selecting the **Show/hide customer information** icon (Windows).
- **Early Payment Discounts:**
  - ✓ Go to Customers > Receive payments.
  - ✓ Enter the customer's payment information.
  - ✓ Select Discount Info (Windows). You can adjust the discount amount here. QuickBooks might suggest a discount based on your payment terms and date.
  - ✓ Specify the account used to track customer discounts.
  - ✓ Click Save. (Mac version might differ)
- **Statement Charge Discounts:** Apply discounts to statement charges by using a **Discount** item in the Accounts Receivable register for the customer (Windows).

By following these steps, you can efficiently record customer payments in QuickBooks for Windows or Mac, maintaining accurate financial records and managing your customer accounts effectively.

# Managing Sales Receipt

Sales receipts are used in QuickBooks Online to record customer payments made at the time of purchase.

Here's a breakdown of how to create, edit, and manage your sales receipts:

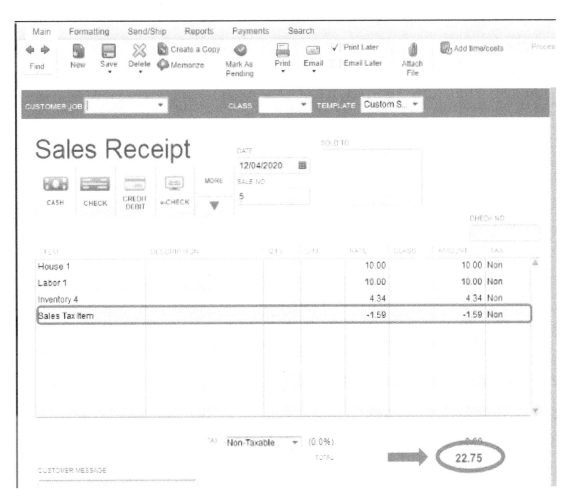

## Creating a Sales Receipt:

1. Go to the **+ New** menu and select **Sales receipt**.

2. From the **Customer** dropdown, choose the customer you're recording the sale for. If the customer is new, click **Add New** to create their profile.

3. (Optional) Enter a **Sales rep** if applicable.

4. In the product/service section, you can either:

    - Select existing items from your product/service list.

    - Click **+ Add New** to create a new item for the sale.

5. Enter the **Quantity** of each item or service sold.

6. The **Rate** (price per unit) will populate automatically if you selected an existing product/service. You can modify the rate if needed.

7. QuickBooks will calculate the **Amount** (quantity x rate) for each line item.

8. (Optional) Add a **Discount** to the entire sale by entering a percentage in the **Discount** field.

9. The **Total** amount of the sales receipt will update automatically based on the line items and any applied discount.

10. You can add a **Memo** at the bottom to include any additional information for the customer.

11. Click **Save** to create the sales receipt.

### Saving and Sending Options:

- **Save:** Saves the sales receipt without sending it to the customer.
- **Save & Send:** Saves the receipt and opens a new email window with the receipt attached for you to send to the customer.
- **Save & Print:** Saves the receipt and allows you to print a physical copy.

### Editing a Sales Receipt:

- Go to the **Sales** menu and select **Sales receipts**.
- Find the sales receipt you want to edit in the list.
- Click the receipt number to open it.
- Make any necessary changes to the sales receipt details.
- Click **Save** to update the receipt.

### Managing Sales Receipts:

- You can search and filter the sales receipt list to locate specific receipts.
- QuickBooks Online allows you to void or delete sales receipts if needed. However, it's generally recommended to void receipts instead of deleting them, as voiding maintains an audit trail.
- You can generate reports based on your sales receipts to analyse your sales trends and customer activity.

## Additional Tips:

- Consider customizing sales receipt templates to include your company logo and branding elements.

- You can integrate your bank account with QuickBooks Online to streamline the process of recording customer payments.
- By enabling email receipts, QuickBooks Online can automatically send a copy of the sales receipt to the customer upon creation.

By understanding how to manage sales receipts in QuickBooks Online, you can efficiently record customer transactions, maintain accurate sales records, and provide a professional experience for your customers.

## Handling Customer Returns and Refunds

QuickBooks Pro Desktop offers functionalities to handle customer returns and process refunds efficiently. Here's an overview of the two primary methods:

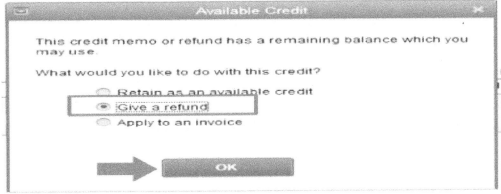

## 1. Using Credit Memos:

This is the most common approach for processing customer returns and issuing refunds in QuickBooks Pro Desktop. Here's a step-by-step guide:

- Go to the Customers menu and select Create Credit Memos/Refunds.

- From the **Customer: Job** dropdown, select the customer who is returning the items and, if applicable, the job associated with the return.
- Enter the **Date** of the credit memo.
- In the item section, you can either:
  - ✓ Select the specific items being returned from your product/service list.
  - ✓ If the return doesn't involve existing inventory items, you can add a new line item with a descriptive name for the returned product or service.
- Enter the quantity of each returned item.
- You can choose a **Reason for Return** from a predefined list or enter a custom reason.
- In the **Refund** section, you have options to:

- **Give a refund:** This allows you to process a cash refund to the customer. QuickBooks will prompt you to specify the payment method (cash, check, etc.) used for the refund.
- **Retain as an available credit:** This creates a credit for the customer's account that they can use towards future purchases.

## 2. Voiding an Invoice:

If the customer has already paid for the items being returned and you want to completely cancel the sale, you can void the original invoice. Here's how:

- Go to the **Customers** menu and select **Customer Centre**.
- Find the invoice associated with the returned items in the customer list.
- Open the invoice by double-clicking on it.
- Click the **Edit** menu and select **Void**.

- QuickBooks will prompt you to confirm voiding the invoice.

**Important Considerations:**

- When using credit memos, ensure you have sufficient inventory on hand (if applicable) to handle the return process.
- If you choose to void an invoice, any payments received for that invoice will need to be refunded to the customer using a separate method (e.g., issuing a check).
- It's advisable to maintain a clear return policy within your business and potentially communicate it to your customers during the sales process.

# Additional Tips:

- QuickBooks allows customizing credit memo templates to include your company logo and return policy information.
- Consider integrating your bank account with QuickBooks to streamline the process of recording refunds issued to customers.
- You can generate reports in QuickBooks to track customer returns and refunds over a specific period.

By understanding these methods and considerations, you can effectively manage customer returns and refunds within QuickBooks Pro Desktop, ensuring accurate record-keeping and customer satisfaction.

# CHAPTER FIVE
# MANAGING VENDORS AND EXPENSES

## Setting Up Vendor Information

Keeping track of your vendors is crucial for efficient expense management and accurate financial reporting. QuickBooks allows you to easily add and manage vendor information, streamlining the process of recording purchases and payments.\

*Here's a breakdown of how to set up vendor information in both QuickBooks Online and QuickBooks Desktop:*

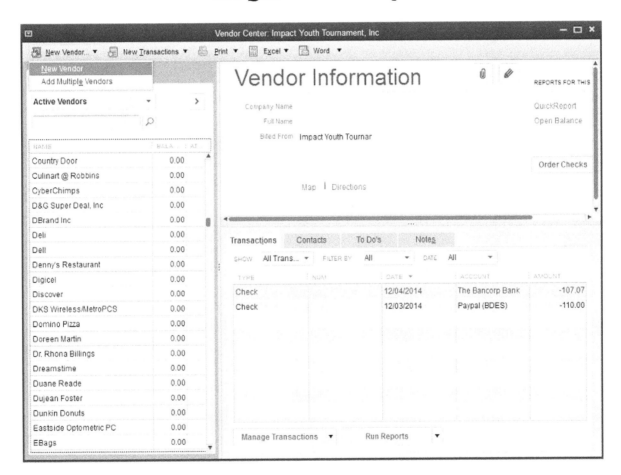

### QuickBooks Online:

1. **Go to Vendors:** Navigate to the **Expenses** menu and select **Vendors** (or use the search bar).

2. **Add New Vendor:** Click the **New vendor** button.

3. **Enter Vendor Details:** Fill out the vendor information form, including:

- **Company Name:** The legal business name of the vendor.
- **Contact Information:** Name, address, phone number, and email address of a contact person at the vendor company.
- **Account Information:** Specify the vendor's account number (if applicable) and the default expense account to use when recording purchases from this vendor.

1. **Optional Details:** You can also include additional information such as:
   - Website address
   - Tax ID number (relevant for tax reporting)
   - Opening balance (any outstanding amount owed to the vendor at the beginning)

2. **Save:** Click **Save** to create the new vendor record.

**QuickBooks Desktop:**

1. **Go to Vendors:** Open the **Vendors** menu and select **Vendors**.
2. **Add New Vendor:** Click the **New** button or select **New Vendor** from the dropdown menu.
3. **Enter Vendor Details:** Similar to QuickBooks Online, fill out the vendor information form, including:
   - **Name:** The legal business name of the vendor.
   - **Contact:** Contact information for the vendor.
   - **Tax Info:** Tax ID number (relevant for tax reporting).
   - **Company Info:** Website address and opening balance.
   - **Other Details:** Additional information like preferred payment method and notes.
4. **Assign Account:** Select the default expense account to be used when recording purchases from this vendor.
5. **Save:** Click **Save** to create the new vendor record.

## Additional Tips:

- **Vendor Management:** QuickBooks allows you to edit, delete, or make inactive existing vendor records as needed.

- **Importing Vendors:** If you have a list of vendors in a spreadsheet, you can import them into QuickBooks for faster setup (available in both Online and Desktop).

- **Vendor Creation During Transactions:** While creating invoices or bills, you can also create new vendors on the fly within QuickBooks.

By following these steps, you can efficiently set up vendor information in QuickBooks, ensuring you have accurate records for all your business expenses. Remember, proper vendor management contributes to streamlined accounting processes and better financial insights.

## Entering Bills

QuickBooks allows you to record transactions for future payment, such as expenses, materials acquired, or services supplied by a vendor. This manner, you can keep track of all your accounts payables and know when a bill needs to be paid.

*Here's a breakdown of the typical steps involved in recording a bill in most accounting software:*

1. **Access Bill Entry:** Locate the section in your accounting software dedicated to managing bills. This might be labelled "Bills," "Accounts Payable," or "Enter Bills" depending on the specific software.

2. **Select Vendor:** Choose the vendor you received the bill from a dropdown list or by searching for their name.

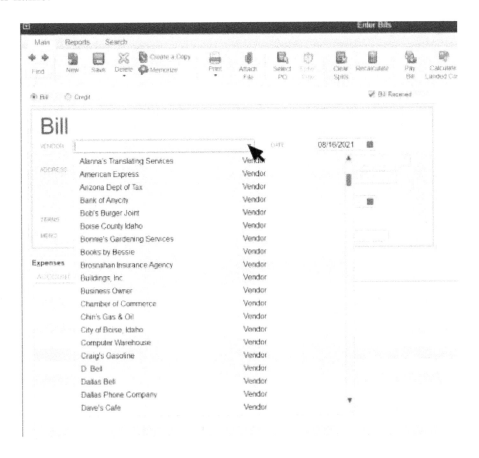

3.  **Enter Bill Details:** Fill in the required information about the bill, typically including:

- **Date:** The date you received the bill.

- **Amount:** The total amount due on the bill.

- **Due Date:** The date by which the payment must be made.

4.  **Bill Type (Optional):** Some software programs let you categorize the bill type. This might be something like "Expenses" for general business costs (rent, utilities) or "Inventory" for items you purchase for resale.

5.  **Save or Create:** Once you've entered all the details, finalize the process by saving the bill or creating a new bill record in your accounting software.

By following these general steps, you can effectively record bills from your vendors in most accounting software programs. Remember to consult your software's specific user guide for detailed instructions or any variations in the process.

## Paying Bills

After you've recorded what you owe your vendors in QuickBooks Desktop, navigate to the Pay Bills window to settle your payables. If you obtained a discount or credit from a vendor, apply it to your bill payment to minimize your total payable.

When paying bills, do not use a check. If you do, the bills stay open and unpaid, resulting in false financial reporting. Here's how to pay your bills properly.

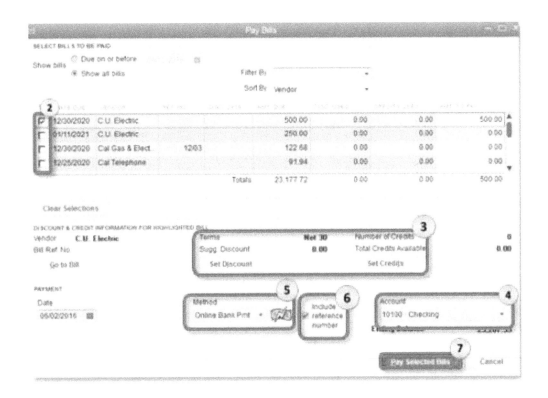

1. **Navigate to the Vendors Menu:**

   - Select **Pay Bills**.

2. **Choose the Account:**

   - From the dropdown, select the appropriate **accounts payable** account.

3. **Select Bills to Pay:**

   - In the table, check the boxes next to the bills you want to pay.

   - **Note:** To mark or unmark all bills, select **Clear Selections** or **Select All Bills**.

4. **Apply Discounts or Credits:**

   - Set any discounts or credits for the bills.

     - **Discount:** Choose this if your vendor provided a discount for the transaction.

     - **Credit:** Choose this if you received a credit from your vendor, reducing the total bill amount.

5. **Enter Payment Details:**

- Specify the date you paid the bill.

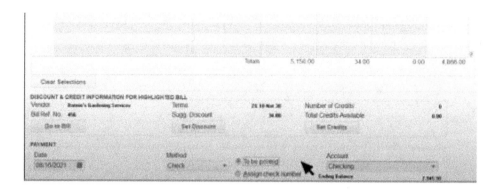

6. Select Payment Method:
   - Check:
   - Choose Assign check number to manually write the check.
   - Choose To be Printed to print the check or add it to the print list.
   - Credit Card:
   - Use credit cards to pay bills, then print a payment stub.
   - Online Bill Payment:
   - Pay your vendor bills directly in QuickBooks. The payment is recorded automatically for accurate reports.
   - Online Bank Payment:
   - The processor prints and mails a check to the employee. Select Include reference number to send the bill or credit reference number with your name and account number.
   - Cash, Debit or ATM card, Paypal, or EFT:
   - Select Check, then Assign check number, even if not paying with an actual check. Enter the payment type in the check number field or leave it blank.

7. Finalize Payment:
   - Select Pay Selected Bills.
   - Choose Done to finish, or Pay More Bills if you have additional bills to pay.

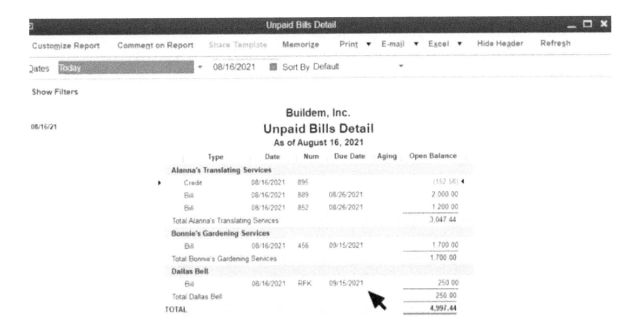

**Additional Information:** Paying bills is part of the usual accounts payable workflow in QuickBooks Desktop. To see the complete list of workflows and other vendor-related transactions, refer to the **Account Payable Workflow**.

## Managing Purchase Orders

Purchase orders (POs) are essential documents used to communicate your intent to buy specific items from a vendor at an agreed-upon price. QuickBooks helps streamline the purchase order process, ensuring clarity and accuracy in your inventory management and financial transactions.

*Here's a breakdown of how to manage purchase orders in both QuickBooks Online and QuickBooks Desktop:*

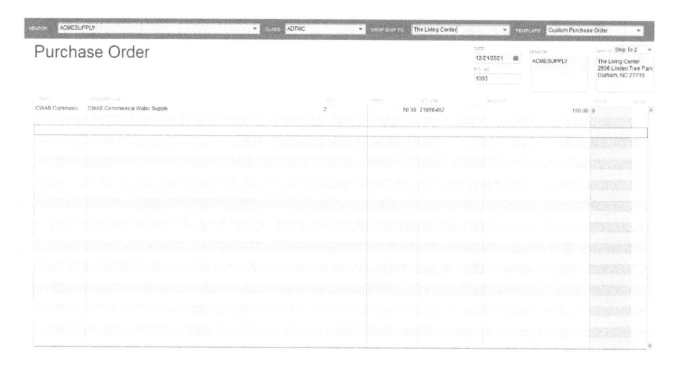

## QuickBooks Online:

### Turning on the Feature (if necessary):

1. Go to **Settings** (gear icon) and select **Accounts and settings**.

2. In the **Expenses** tab, locate the **Purchase orders** section.

3. Activate the **Use purchase orders** option (if not already enabled).

4. (Optional) You can define custom fields and a default message for your purchase orders in this section.

### Creating a Purchase Order:

1. Click the Plus (+) sign and select Purchase order.

2. Choose the vendor you're placing the order with from the Vendor dropdown list.

3. Review the Mailing address and update the Ship to address if necessary (where the items will be delivered).

4. Enter the Purchase Order date.

5. In the Item details section, add the products or services you're ordering. Specify the quantity, description, unit price, and any relevant details.

6. Click Save to create the purchase order. You can also choose Save and send to electronically transmit the PO to the vendor.

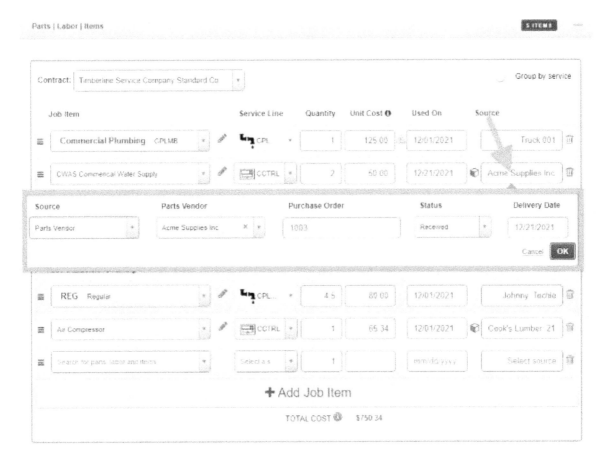

## Managing Existing Purchase Orders:

- You can view, edit, or delete purchase orders you've created.
- Once you receive the ordered items, you can convert the purchase order into a bill for payment purposes.

# QuickBooks Desktop:

## Turning on the Feature (if necessary):

1. Go to **Edit** menu and select **Preferences**.
2. Choose **Items & Inventory** and then the **Company Preferences** tab.
3. Check the **Inventory and purchase orders are active** checkbox and select **OK**.

## Creating a Purchase Order:

1. Go to Vendors and select Create Purchase Orders.
2. Click Create Purchase Order....
3. Fill out the details, including vendor, shipping information, and purchase order date.

4. In the Items section, add the products or services you're ordering. Specify the quantity, description, and unit price.

5. Click Save to create the purchase order.

<u>**Managing Existing Purchase Orders:**</u>

- Similar to QuickBooks Online, you can view, edit, or delete purchase orders.

- When you receive the items, you can record them in QuickBooks and link them to the corresponding purchase order.

<u>**Benefits of Using Purchase Orders:**</u>

- **Improved Communication:** Purchase orders provide a clear and formal document outlining your order details to the vendor.

- **Inventory Management:** Helps track what you've ordered and expected delivery dates, ensuring better inventory control.

- **Cost Control:** Helps you lock in agreed-upon prices with vendors and avoid potential misunderstandings.

- **Streamlined Bill Creation:** Simplifies the process of converting purchase orders into bills for payment when items are received.

By understanding how to manage purchase orders in QuickBooks, you can enhance your procurement process, gain better control over your inventory, and ensure accurate financial records. Remember, consulting your accountant can provide guidance on best practices for purchase order use within your business.

# Tracking Expenses

Efficient expense tracking is essential for any business. QuickBooks offers multiple functionalities to help you record, categorize, and analyse your business expenditures.

*Here's a breakdown of key methods for tracking expenses in both QuickBooks Online and QuickBooks Desktop:*

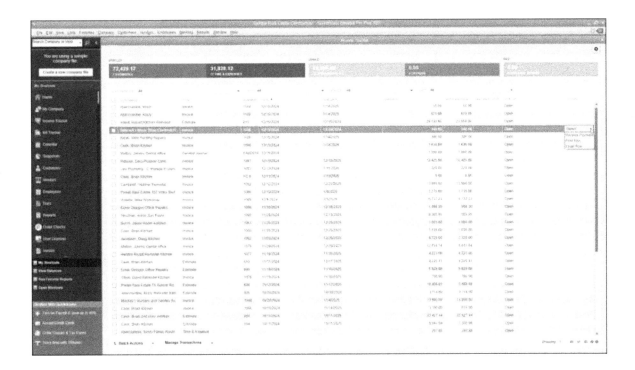

## Entering Expenses:

- **Manual Entry:** This involves manually entering each expense transaction into QuickBooks. You'll typically specify the date, payee (vendor), amount, expense category, and payment method.

- **Bank Feed Integration:** Connect your bank accounts to QuickBooks to automatically import your bank transactions. You can then categorize and edit these imported transactions as needed.

- **Mobile App:** Use the QuickBooks mobile app to capture receipts on the go. The app can extract expense data from receipt images, allowing you to easily record expenses while you're out.

## Categorizing Expenses:

- **Expense Categories:** QuickBooks provides a predefined chart of accounts with expense categories. Choose the most appropriate category for each expense to group similar expenditures. You can also create custom categories to suit your specific needs.

## Managing Bills:

- **Bill Entry:** For recurring expenses like rent or utilities, you can create bills in QuickBooks. This allows you to schedule bill payments and track due dates.

58

### Reconciling Accounts:

- Regularly reconcile your bank statements with your QuickBooks account to ensure all transactions are recorded accurately. This helps identify any discrepancies and maintain data integrity.

### Reports:

**Generate Reports:** QuickBooks offers various reports to analyse your expenses. These reports can help you identify spending trends, track specific categories, and gain insights into your overall financial health. Common expense reports include:

- Profit and Loss Statement: Summarizes your income and expenses over a period.
- Expenses by Vendor: Shows a breakdown of spending by each vendor.
- Expenses by Category: Categorizes your total expenses for a period.

## Additional Tips:

- Develop a consistent system for tracking expenses. Choose a method (manual entry, bank feed, mobile app) that works best for your business.
- Maintain a clear and organized filing system for physical receipts, especially for tax purposes.
- Regularly review your expense reports to identify areas for cost savings or budgeting adjustments.

By following these practices and leveraging the tools available in QuickBooks, you can effectively track your business expenses, gain valuable financial insights, and make informed financial decisions. Remember, consulting your accountant can provide guidance on best practices for expense tracking specific to your business.

## Handling Vendor Credits and Refunds

When a vendor issues you a credit or refund for a purchase, it's important to record it accurately in QuickBooks to maintain financial clarity. Here's how to handle vendor credits and refunds in both QuickBooks Online and QuickBooks Desktop:

### QuickBooks Online:

There are two main approaches to recording vendor credits and refunds in QuickBooks Online:

### 1. Vendor Credit:

This is suitable when the vendor issues a credit for a returned item or a price adjustment.

#### Steps:

1. Go to **Vendors** and select the vendor that issued the credit.
2. Click on **New** and choose **Vendor credit**.
3. Enter the credit amount and select the expense account used for the original purchase.
4. (Optional) Add a brief explanation for the credit in the Memo field.
5. Click **Save** to record the vendor credit.

### 2. Credit Card Credit:

This is appropriate when a refund is issued directly to your credit card for a purchase.

#### Steps:

1. Go to **Banking** and select the credit card used for the purchase.
2. Click on **New transaction** and choose **Credit card credit**.
3. Select the vendor from the payee dropdown list.
4. Enter the credit amount, payment date, and (optional) a brief explanation in the Memo field.
5. Click **Save** to record the credit card credit.

### QuickBooks Desktop:

QuickBooks Desktop offers a similar approach to recording vendor credits:

#### Steps:

1. Go to **Vendors** and select **Enter Bills**.
2. Click the **Credit** radio button instead of the usual "Pay Bill" option.
3. Select the vendor from the dropdown list.
4. Enter the credit amount and choose the expense account used for the original purchase.
5. (Optional) Add a brief explanation for the credit in the Memo field.
6. Click **Save & Close** to record the vendor credit.

## Important Notes:

- Regardless of the method used, ensure the credit amount matches the amount you received from the vendor.

- Properly matching the credit to the original purchase ensures accurate tracking of your accounts payable and expenses.
- Consult your accountant for guidance on handling complex vendor credits or refunds, especially those involving tax implications.

By understanding these approaches, you can effectively record vendor credits and refunds in QuickBooks, maintaining accurate financial records and streamlining your accounts payable processes.

# CHAPTER SIX
# BANKING

## Connecting to Bank Account

Connecting your bank account to QuickBooks offers several advantages, including:

- **Automatic Transaction Download:** Eliminate manual data entry by automatically importing your bank transactions into QuickBooks.

- **Improved Accuracy:** Reduce the risk of errors associated with manual data entry.

- **Streamlined Reconciliation:** Simplifies the process of reconciling your bank statements with your QuickBooks account.

- **Enhanced Cash Flow Management:** Gain real-time insights into your cash flow by having your bank account data readily available in QuickBooks.

Here's a breakdown of the general steps involved in connecting your bank account to QuickBooks, applicable to both QuickBooks Online and QuickBooks Desktop (with slight variations):

### 1. Accessing Bank Connection:

**QuickBooks Online:** Go to the **Banking** menu or find the **Bank Feed** section within QuickBooks Online.

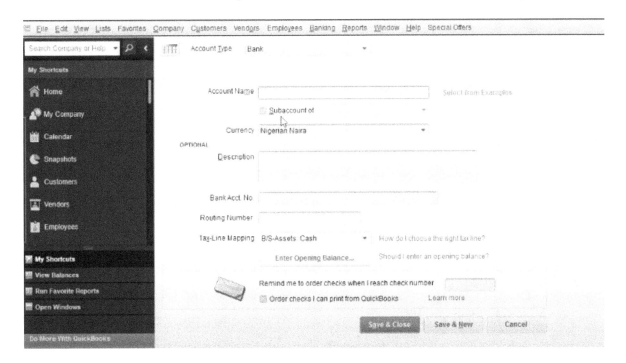

QuickBooks Desktop: Navigate to the Banking menu and select Connect Bank Account.

## 2. Selecting Your Bank:

- A search bar or list will be available where you can enter your bank's name.
- Choose your bank from the displayed options.

## 3. Secure Login Credentials:

- You'll be redirected to your bank's secure login page.
- Enter your online banking username and password to securely connect QuickBooks to your bank account.

## 4. Account Selection (if applicable):

- Depending on your bank and setup, you might need to select the specific bank account(s) you want to connect to QuickBooks.

## 5. Downloading Transactions:

- Once connected, you can initiate the download of your bank transactions into QuickBooks. This might involve specifying a date range for the transactions you want to import.

## 6. Categorization (Optional):

- QuickBooks might attempt to automatically categorize your downloaded transactions. You can review and adjust these categories as needed to ensure accurate expense tracking.

# Important Notes:

- **Security:** The bank connection process uses secure protocols to safeguard your online banking credentials. QuickBooks itself doesn't store your bank login information.
- **Two-Factor Authentication:** If your bank utilizes two-factor authentication, you might need to provide an additional verification code during the connection process.
- **Data Accuracy:** Double-check the downloaded transactions for accuracy and categorize them appropriately.
- **Account Limitations:** Some bank accounts or account types might not be compatible with online banking connections.

By following these general steps and considering the important notes, you can successfully connect your bank account to QuickBooks and enjoy the benefits of automated transaction downloads and improved financial management. Remember, if you encounter any difficulties during the connection process, consult your bank or refer to QuickBooks' specific support resources.

## Recording Bank Deposits

Recording your bank deposits in QuickBooks ensures your financial records accurately reflect the money coming into your business. Here's a breakdown of the process in both QuickBooks Online and QuickBooks Desktop:

### QuickBooks Online:

1. **Go to Banking:** Locate the **Banking** menu or find the **Make a Deposit** option within QuickBooks Online.
2. **Select Deposit Method:** Choose the deposit method that reflects how you deposited the funds (e.g., "At the bank," "Online banking deposit").
3. **Select Account:** Specify the bank account where you deposited the funds.
4. **Add Deposits (optional):** You can either:
    - **Manually Add Funds:** Enter the deposit details like date, amount, and memo (optional).
    - **Select Transactions to Deposit:** If you've already recorded the deposits as income transactions (sales receipts, invoices), you can choose them from a list to combine them into a single bank deposit.
5. **Review and Save:** Double-check the deposit details and ensure the total matches your deposit slip. Click **Save** to record the bank deposit.

### QuickBooks Desktop:

1. Go to Make Deposits: Navigate to the Banking menu and select Make Deposits.
2. Payments to Deposit: In the Payments to Deposit window, you'll see a list of your outstanding customer payments (invoices, sales receipts).
3. Select Deposits: Choose the payments you want to include in this bank deposit by checking the boxes next to them.
4. Deposit To: Select the bank account where you deposited the funds.
5. Deposit Total: Verify that the total displayed matches your deposit slip.
6. Deposit Date: Enter the date you made the deposit at the bank.
7. Memo (Optional): Add a brief memo for reference purposes (optional).

8. **Save & Close:** Click Save & Close to record the bank deposit.

## Additional Tips:

- **Reconcile Regularly:** Regularly reconcile your bank statements with your QuickBooks account to ensure all deposits and withdrawals are accurately recorded.

- **Undeposited Funds Account (Optional):** If you frequently make deposits that combine multiple customer payments, consider using the "Undeposited Funds" account as a temporary holding account before recording the final bank deposit.

- **Duplicate Deposits:** Be cautious when recording deposits to avoid duplicates. Ensure each deposit is recorded only once.

By following these steps and considering the additional tips, you can efficiently record your bank deposits in QuickBooks, maintaining accurate and up-to-date financial records for your business. Remember, consult your accountant if you have any questions or require specific guidance on handling bank deposits in QuickBooks.

## Reconciling Bank Accounts

Just like balancing your check book, you should inspect your QuickBooks accounts to ensure they match your actual bank and credit card bills. The technique is known as reconciling.

It is advised that you reconcile your bank, savings, and credit card accounts every month. Once you receive your bank statements, compare the list of transactions to what you entered into QuickBooks. If everything matches, it means your accounts are balanced and accurate.

### Step 1: Check your opening balance.

Before you begin reconciliation, make sure to back up your firm file.

If you're reconciling an account for the first time, check the opening balance.

### Step 2: Prepare for the Reconciliation

Ensure all transactions for the bank statement period you plan to reconcile are entered. If there are transactions that haven't cleared the bank and aren't on your statement, wait to enter them.

### Step 3: Start Your Reconciliation

Once you receive your bank statement, you can begin the reconciliation process.

- **Multiple Months:** If reconciling multiple months, start with the oldest bank statement and reconcile each month separately, one statement at a time.

**Important:** For reconciling a Merchant or Payments account, if QuickBooks Desktop detects that you aren't signed in, a sign-in window will appear. This ensures your account is linked to a valid company ID.

1. Go to the Banking Menu:
   - Select Reconcile.
2. Select the Account:
   - In the Account field, choose the bank or credit card account you want to reconcile.
3. Verify Statement Date:
   - The **Statement Date** is automatically filled in, typically 30 or 31 days after the previous reconciliation's statement date. Adjust it as needed to match your bank statement.
4. Verify Beginning Balance:
   - QuickBooks automatically enters the **Beginning Balance** using the ending balance from your last reconciliation.
5. Enter Ending Balance:
   - Input the **Ending Balance** from your bank statement.
6. Enter Additional Charges:
   - Add the **Service Charge** and **Interest Earned** from your bank statement. Do not enter charges already recorded in QuickBooks.
7. Review and Continue:
   - Review the fields for accuracy. If everything is correct, select **Continue** or **OK**.


## Troubleshooting:

**Mismatched Balances:** If your beginning balance doesn't match your statement, use the following tools:

- **Locate Discrepancies:** Provides reports to find discrepancies and other reconciliation issues.
- **Fixing Balances:** Instructions on how to fix your opening and beginning balances.

Starting Over:

- Select **Undo Last Reconciliation** to revert your beginning balance to the previous reconciliation's beginning balance. All cleared transactions will become uncleared.

## Step 4: Compare Your Bank Statement and QuickBooks

To reconcile, compare the transactions on your bank statement with those in QuickBooks.

### Preparation Tips:

- Hide Future Transactions: Select Hide transactions after the statement's end date to focus on the statement period.
- Credit Card Accounts: Work on one section at a time, such as Charges and Cash Advances (purchases) and Payments and Credits (payments to the credit card company).
- Online Banking Accounts: Select Matched and enter the Statement Ending Date to automatically select matched transactions. Note: Matched transactions have a lightning bolt icon that changes to a checkmark after reconciliation.
- Sorting Transactions: To sort, select the header or title of a column. If there are more transactions in QuickBooks than on your bank statement, resort the list.

### Matching Your Transactions:

- **Start with the First Transaction:** Begin with the first transaction on your bank statement and find it in the Reconciliation window in QuickBooks.
- **Compare Transactions:** If the transactions match, put a checkmark in the checkmark column to reconcile the transaction.
- **Clearing Transactions:** As you reconcile transactions, the Cleared Balance amount decreases. It increases if you clear deposits and other credits.
- **Unmatched Transactions:** If a transaction doesn't appear on your statement, do not mark it as reconciled.

### Quick Matching Checks:

- **Summary Comparison:** Check the **Items you've marked cleared** section for the total number and amount of transactions. Compare this with your bank statement to ensure nothing is missing.
- **Editing Transactions:** To edit or get more info about a transaction, select the transaction and then **Go To** or double-click it.

- **Modifying Info:** If you need to change info from Step 3, select **Modify**. This section shows the service charges, interest, and ending balance.

<u>Completing the Reconciliation:</u>
- **Difference Should Be $0.00:** When you finish, the difference between your bank statement and QuickBooks should be $0.00. If it is, select **Reconcile no**

# Managing Credit Card Transactions

Managing credit card transactions in QuickBooks is essential for accurate expense tracking and maintaining a clear overview of your business finances.

*Here's a breakdown of how to handle credit card transactions in both QuickBooks Online and QuickBooks Desktop:*

<u>QuickBooks Online:</u>

There are two main approaches to manage credit card transactions in QuickBooks Online:

<u>1. Automatic Download (Bank Feed):</u>
- **Connect your credit card account:** Enable the bank feed feature and connect your credit card account to QuickBooks Online. This allows for automatic download of your credit card transactions.
- **Categorize Transactions:** Once downloaded, review and categorize these transactions appropriately. You can assign expense categories for each transaction based on the purchase details.

<u>2. Manual Entry:</u>
- If automatic download isn't available or for specific transactions, you can enter them manually.
- **Steps:** Go to the **Banking** menu or find the **Add a bank transaction** option.
  - ✓ **Select Account:** Choose the credit card account associated with the transaction.
  - ✓ **Transaction Date:** Enter the date the purchase was made.
  - ✓ **Amount:** Enter the transaction amount (negative value).
  - ✓ **Payee:** Enter the payee name from the credit card statement.
  - ✓ **Category:** Choose the appropriate expense category for the purchase.

✓ **Memo (Optional):** Add a brief description of the purchase.

✓ **Save:** Click **Save** to record the credit card transaction.

# QuickBooks Desktop:

Here's how to record a credit card transaction in QuickBooks Desktop:

## Steps:

1. Go to Banking menu and select Enter Credit Card Transactions.
2. Select the appropriate credit card account from the Account dropdown.
3. Enter the Date of the transaction.
4. Enter the Payee name from your credit card statement.
5. Enter the Amount of the transaction (negative value).
6. Choose the relevant expense Category for the purchase.
7. Add a brief Memo for reference (optional).
8. Click Save & Close to record the credit card transaction.

### Reconciling Credit Card Statements:

Regularly reconcile your credit card statements with your QuickBooks account. This ensures all transactions are accurately recorded and categorized.

# Additional Tips:

- **Pay Down Credit Card Debt:** Consider setting up a transfer to pay down your credit card balance regularly from your checking account within QuickBooks.

- **Track Reward Points (Optional):** If your credit card offers rewards programs, you can utilize a separate account in QuickBooks to track your accumulated points (consult your accountant for guidance).

By following these approaches and considering the additional tips, you can effectively manage your credit card transactions in QuickBooks. This ensures accurate expense tracking, better financial insights, and informed financial decisions for your business.

Remember, consulting your accountant can provide guidance on best practices for managing credit card transactions specific to your business and tax situation

# Handling Bank Fees and Charges

Bank fees and service charges are a common business expense. Recording them accurately in QuickBooks ensures your financial records reflect your true income and expenses.

*Here's how to handle bank fees and charges in both QuickBooks Online and QuickBooks Desktop:*

## QuickBooks Online:

There are two main approaches to record bank fees in QuickBooks Online:

### 1. Using the Bank Feed:

- When you connect your bank account and download transactions, bank fees might automatically be downloaded along with your other bank statements.
- **Review:** Carefully review these downloaded transactions and categorize them as "Bank service charges" or a similar expense category.

### 2. Manual Entry:

- If a bank fee isn't automatically downloaded, you can add it manually.
- **Steps:** Go to the **Banking** menu or find the **Add a bank transaction** option.
  - ✓ **Select Account:** Choose the bank account where the fee was deducted.
  - ✓ **Transaction Date:** Enter the date the fee was incurred.
  - ✓ **Amount:** Enter the amount of the bank fee (negative value).
  - ✓ **Payee:** Select an appropriate payee, such as "Bank Fees" or the name of your bank.
  - ✓ **Category:** Choose "Bank service charges" or a similar expense category.
  - ✓ **Memo (Optional):** Add a brief description of the fee (e.g., "Monthly service charge").
  - ✓ **Save:** Click **Save** to record the bank fee.

## QuickBooks Desktop:

Here's how to record a bank fee in QuickBooks Desktop:

### Steps:

1. Go to **Banking** menu and select **Write Checks**.
2. Select the bank account where the fee was deducted from the **Account** dropdown.
3. Enter a **Check number** (you can use a unique identifier for bank fees).
4. Leave the **Pay to the order of** field blank.

5. Enter the **Date** the fee was incurred.

6. Enter the **amount** of the bank fee (negative value).

7. Choose "Bank service charges" or a similar expense category from the **Expense** account dropdown.

8. Add a brief memo for reference in the **Memo** field (optional).

9. Click **Save & Close** to record the bank fee.

## Important Notes:

- **Matching Downloaded Transactions:** If you use the bank feed and encounter downloaded bank fees with unclear descriptions, you might need to match them to the corresponding entries in your bank statement for accurate categorization.

- **Reconciliation:** Regularly reconcile your bank statements with your QuickBooks account to ensure all bank fees are recorded and categorized correctly.

By understanding these methods, you can effectively handle bank fees and charges in QuickBooks, maintaining accurate financial records and proper expense tracking. Remember, consulting your accountant can provide guidance on best practices for handling bank fees specific to your business.

# CHAPTER SEVEN
# PAYROLL

## Setting Up Payroll in QuickBooks

As a small business owner, paying your employees correctly is one of your most important responsibilities. To ensure accuracy and compliance with legal requirements, you need reliable payroll software.

While basic payroll can be managed manually, using software like QuickBooks Payroll powered by Employment Hero simplifies the process and allows you to handle payroll efficiently in-house.

After signing up for QuickBooks, the next step is to connect to QuickBooks Payroll. Here are a few easy steps to set up your payroll, but first, gather the following details:

- Company Information: Including your ABN (Australian Business Number).
- Employee Information: Including TFN (Tax File Number), superannuation, and bank details.
- Pay History: If you've already paid employees in the current year.
- Bank Details: For setting up ABA files and superannuation payments.

With this information ready, follow the steps below to finalize your payroll setup and get closer to completing your first pay run.

**Step 1:** Navigate to the Payroll tab on the left navigation bar.

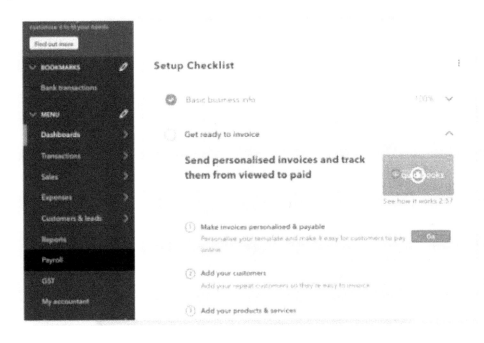

**Step 2:** Enter your ABN, business name, and address.

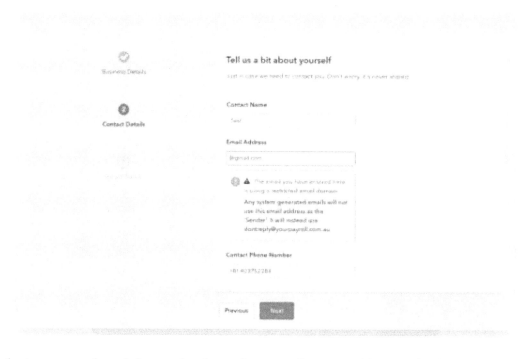

**Step 3:** Enter your contact information, including name, email address, and phone number.

**Step 4:** Select your usual work hours, the days of your ordinary working week, the frequency with which you process a pay run, and the industry you work in.

73

**Step 5:** Sign Up is the initial step in setting up payroll.

# Adding Employees

Adding employees in QuickBooks ensures you can process payroll, track work hours, and maintain accurate employee records.

*Here's a breakdown of the process for adding employees in both QuickBooks Online and QuickBooks Desktop:*

<u>**QuickBooks Online:**</u>

1. **Go to Payroll Centre:** Navigate to the **Employees** section within QuickBooks Online. It might be labelled **Payroll Centre** or similar wording depending on your version.

2. **Add Employee:** Locate the **Add Employee** button or option.

3. **Enter Employee Information:** Fill in the employee's basic details like name, contact information, address, and date of birth.

4. **Setup Payroll Details (Optional):** You can set up payroll details like pay method (salary, hourly), pay rate, and start date.

How often do you pay Karen?

Every Week  ▼

When's the next payday?

10/28/2016

When's the last day of work (pay period) for that payday?

10/28/2016

What do you want to name this pay schedule?

Friday

☐ Use this schedule for employees you add after Karen

5. **Enable Employee Self Service (Optional):** QuickBooks Online allows you to invite employees to set up their own direct deposit information and tax withholding through a secure portal.

6. **Review and Save:** Double-check the information you entered and click **Save** to add the employee.

# QuickBooks Desktop:

1. **Go to Employees Menu:** Click on the **Employees** menu within QuickBooks Desktop.

2. **New Employee:** Select **New Employee** from the menu options.

3. **Employee Information:** Enter the employee's basic details like name, contact information, address, and social security number (or equivalent for your location).

4. **Payroll Info:** Set up payroll details like pay method, pay rate, and pay schedule. You can also specify tax information and deductions here.

5. **Additional Details (Optional):** Fill in any additional employee details such as hire date, termination date (if applicable), and emergency contact information.

6. **Save & Close:** Review the employee information and click **Save & Close** to add the employee.

# Additional Tips:

- **Employee Permissions (QuickBooks Online):** Manage user permissions to control which employees can access payroll information.

- **Tax Forms:** Use QuickBooks to generate and submit tax forms for your employees (e.g., W-2s). Consult your accountant for guidance on tax-related matters.

- **Employee Termination (Optional):** If you need to terminate an employee, QuickBooks can help you with the process in terms of payroll and final payments.

By following these steps, you can add employees in QuickBooks and maintain organized employee records. Remember, consulting your accountant is recommended to ensure you're setting up payroll and taxes correctly for your business and employees.

## Processing Payroll

Processing payroll involves calculating employee wages, withholding taxes and deductions, and generating paychecks or direct deposits. QuickBooks offers a streamlined way to handle payroll for your employees.

### *Here's a breakdown of the general steps for processing payroll in both QuickBooks Online and QuickBooks Desktop:*

<u>Before you begin:</u>

- Ensure you have added all your employees to QuickBooks with their payroll information (pay rate, pay method, etc.) set up.
- Have your latest tax tables downloaded into QuickBooks.

## Processing Payroll:

### QuickBooks Online:

1. **Go to Payroll Centre:** Navigate to the **Payroll** section or **Payroll Centre** in QuickBooks Online.
2. **Select Pay Period:** Choose the appropriate pay period for which you want to process payroll (e.g., weekly, bi-weekly, monthly).
3. **Review Employee Details:** QuickBooks might automatically populate employee hours based on timesheets or previous entries. You can review and edit these hours if needed.
4. **Preview Payroll:** Once you've reviewed employee hours and pay details, preview the payroll to see the net pay for each employee after taxes and deductions are withheld.
5. **Pay Employees:** Choose to pay employees either by direct deposit (if set up) or by printing checks. QuickBooks will guide you through the steps for each payment method.
6. **Submit Payroll (Optional):** Depending on your QuickBooks Online subscription, you might have the option to submit payroll information directly to a payroll service provider for processing and tax filing.

1. **Go to Payroll Menu:** Click on the **Payroll** menu within QuickBooks Desktop.

2. **Run Payroll:** Select **Run Payroll** from the menu options.

3. **Select Pay Period:** Choose the appropriate pay period for which you want to process payroll.

4. **Review Employee Details:** Similar to QuickBooks Online, review employee hours and make any necessary edits.

5. **Calculate Payroll:** Click on **Calculate Payroll** to process payroll taxes and deductions based on your settings and employee information.

6. **Preview Payroll:** Review the calculated net pay for each employee before finalizing the payroll process.

7. **Pay Employees:** Choose to pay employees by direct deposit (if set up) or by printing checks. QuickBooks Desktop will guide you through the steps for each method.

By understanding these steps and considerations, you can effectively process payroll for your employees in QuickBooks. Remember, consulting your accountant is recommended to ensure you're following proper payroll procedures and tax regulations for your business location.

## Managing Payroll Taxes

QuickBooks can help you manage payroll taxes efficiently by automating calculations, tracking liabilities, and facilitating payments and filings (in some cases).

*Here's a breakdown of managing payroll taxes in both QuickBooks Online and QuickBooks Desktop:*

Understanding Payroll Taxes:

There are typically three main types of payroll taxes to consider:

- **Social Security and Medicare:** These are federal taxes withheld from employee paychecks and matched by the employer. The combined employer and employee contribution rates are subject to change, so stay updated.

- **Federal Unemployment Tax (FUTA):** A federal tax paid by employers solely to fund unemployment benefits.

- **State and Local Taxes:** These vary by location and might include state income tax, unemployment insurance, and disability taxes.

<u>**QuickBooks Online:**</u>

- **Automatic Calculations:** QuickBooks Online automatically calculates payroll taxes based on your location and employee information.
- **Track Tax Liabilities:** View your total payroll tax liabilities within QuickBooks reports. These reports show you the amount of taxes owed for each tax type (Social Security, Medicare, FUTA, etc.).
- **Pay Taxes (Optional):** Depending on your subscription level, QuickBooks Online may offer integrated tax payments. You can electronically pay federal and state payroll taxes directly through QuickBooks.
- **E-file Forms (Optional):** Similar to tax payments, some versions of QuickBooks Online allow electronic filing of tax forms (e.g., Form 941) directly within the software.

<u>**QuickBooks Desktop:**</u>

1. **Manual Calculations (Optional):** While QuickBooks Desktop can calculate payroll taxes, it might require some manual setup to ensure accuracy. You might need to enter tax rates and filing thresholds.
2. **Tax Liability Reports:** Similar to QuickBooks Online, you can access reports that show your outstanding payroll tax liabilities.
3. **Tax Payments:** You'll need to make tax payments to the IRS and relevant state/local authorities separately from QuickBooks Desktop.
4. **E-filing Forms (Optional):** Some versions of QuickBooks Desktop allow electronic filing of tax forms, but you might need to purchase an additional payroll service.

## Important Notes:

- **Tax Updates:** Ensure you keep your payroll tax rates and filing thresholds updated within QuickBooks to maintain accuracy.
- **Consult Your Accountant:** While QuickBooks can automate calculations and simplify tax management, consulting a qualified accountant is highly recommended. They can guide you on tax compliance, filing requirements, and any specific tax implications for your business.

- **State and Local Variations:** Payroll tax regulations can vary by state and locality. Be sure to research and comply with specific requirements for your business location.

# Additional Tips:

- **Separate Tax Accounts:** Set up separate accounts in your chart of accounts for tracking payroll tax liabilities. This helps maintain clear records and simplifies reconciliation.
- **Schedule Tax Payments:** Plan ahead and schedule tax payments to avoid penalties for late filing or payment.

By effectively managing payroll taxes in QuickBooks and consulting your accountant, you can ensure your business stays compliant with tax regulations and avoids any potential tax-related issues.

# Printing Pay checks and Stubs

## QuickBooks Online Payroll

### Step 1: Set Up Your Printing Preferences

1. **Access Payroll Settings:**

   - Go to **Settings** ⚙, then select **Payroll settings**.

2. **Edit Printing Preferences:**

   - In the **Printing** section, select **Edit** ✎.

   - Choose your preferred printing option:

     - **Pay stubs on plain paper**

     - **Paycheques on QuickBooks-compatible cheque paper:** Select the type of voucher (Print paycheque plus 1 pay stub or Print paycheque plus 2 pay stubs). Then select **Align my printer** to set up alignment.

   - Select **Save**.

3. **Printer Alignment:**

   - On the **Printer Setup** page, follow the on-screen steps.

- Select **Save**.

- When finished, select **Done**.

- **Note:** You can also access printing preferences after creating payroll by selecting **Change print settings** in the **Payroll is done** window.

For more information, see how to fix print alignment for preprinted cheques.

**Step 2: Print Paycheques or Pay Stubs**

1. **Navigate to Payroll:**

   - Go to **Payroll** and select **Employees** (Take me there).

2. **Select Paycheques:**

   - Select **Paycheque list** below **Run payroll**.

   - Choose the paycheque you want to print. Use **Filter▼** to change the date range or employee if needed.

3. **Print:**

   - In the **Action** column, select **Print**.

   - A preview of the paycheque or pay stub will open. Select the printer icon to print.

## QuickBooks Desktop Payroll
**Step 1: Set Up Your Printing Preferences**

**Set Up Paycheques:**

1. **Printer Setup:**

   - Navigate to **File**, then select **Printer Setup**.

   - Select **Cheque/Paycheque** from the **Form Name ▼** drop-down menu.

2. **Configure Printer:**

   - Select the **Settings** tab.

   - Choose your **Printer Name** and **Printer Type**.

- Set your **Check Style** to Voucher, Standard, or Wallet.

- Select additional options to print your company name and address, logo, or image.

- Select **OK**.

**Set Up Pay Stubs:**

**Printer Setup:**

- Navigate to **File**, then select **Printer Setup**.

- Select **Pay stub** from the **Form Name** ▼ drop-down menu.

2. **Configure Printer:**

- Choose your **Printer Name** and **Printer Type**.

- Select **OK**.

**Step 2: Print Paycheques or Pay Stubs**

**Print Paycheques:**

1. **Navigate to Print Forms:**

- Go to **File**, then select **Print Forms**.

- Select **Pay Cheques**.

2. **Select Payroll Account:**

- Choose your payroll **Bank Account** ▼.

- Ensure the number in the **First Cheque Number** field matches the first cheque in your printer.

3. **Print:**

- Select the paycheques to print.

- Select **OK**.

- Review your print settings, then select **Print**.

**Print Pay Stubs:**

1. **Navigate to Print Forms:**

   - Go to **File**, then select **Print Forms**.

   - Select **Pay stubs**.

2. **Select Payroll Account:**

   - Choose your payroll **Bank Account ▼**.

   - Enter the date range that includes the pay date of the pay stubs.

   - Select the pay stubs you want to print. Use the **Employee ▼** filter for specific employees if needed.

3. **Preferences and Print:**

   - Select **Preferences** to choose the company and employee info that prints on the pay stubs.

   - Enter a message in the **Company message to be printed** box if desired.

   - Select **Preview** to view pay stubs before printing.

   - Select **Print**.

# Handling Payroll Liabilities

QuickBooks helps manage payroll liabilities by streamlining calculations, tracking what you owe in taxes, and facilitating payments. Here's a breakdown of handling payroll liabilities in both QuickBooks Online and QuickBooks Desktop:

**Understanding Payroll Liabilities:**

- Payroll liabilities represent the total amount of taxes you owe to federal, state, and local tax authorities on behalf of your employees.

- These taxes are typically withheld from employee paychecks throughout a pay period. The employer is responsible for remitting these withheld taxes along with their own share of payroll taxes to the appropriate authorities.

## QuickBooks Online:

- **Automatic Calculations:** QuickBooks Online automatically calculates payroll taxes based on your location and employee information.
- **Track Liabilities:** View your total payroll tax liabilities within dedicated reports. These reports categorize the amount you owe for each tax type (Social Security, Medicare, FUTA, etc.).
- **Pay Liabilities:** QuickBooks Online allows you to easily pay your payroll liabilities electronically through the software (depending on your subscription). You can schedule payments to ensure timely remittance.

### *Here's how to pay liabilities in QuickBooks Online:*

- Navigate to the **Taxes** section (might be under **Payroll Centre**).
- Select the **Pay Liabilities** tab.
- Choose the date range for the liabilities you want to pay.
- Select the bank account you want to use for the payment.
- Review the payment details and click **Create** to generate the liability checks or initiate electronic payments.

## QuickBooks Desktop:

1. **Calculations:** Similar to Online, QuickBooks Desktop calculates payroll taxes. You might need some initial setup to ensure accuracy (tax rates, filing thresholds).
2. **Track Liabilities:** Access reports that display your outstanding payroll tax liabilities.
3. **Pay Liabilities:** Unlike Online, you'll need to make tax payments to the IRS and relevant state/local authorities separately from QuickBooks Desktop.

### *Here's how to pay liabilities in QuickBooks Desktop:*

- Go to the Employees menu and choose Payroll Liabilities followed by Pay Payroll Liabilities.
- Select the date range for the liabilities you want to pay.
- Choose the bank account you want to use for the payment.
- Review the payment details and click Create to generate liability checks.

## Important Notes:

- **Timely Payments:** Ensure you make tax payments on time to avoid penalties for late filing or payment. Schedule payments in advance using QuickBooks reminders (Online) or set calendar reminders (Desktop).

- **Accountant's Role:** While QuickBooks automates calculations, consulting a qualified accountant is recommended. They can advise on tax compliance, filing requirements, and any specific tax implications for your business.

## Additional Tips:

- **Separate Accounts:** Set up separate accounts in your chart of accounts for tracking payroll tax liabilities. This helps maintain clear records and simplifies reconciliation.

- **Review Reports:** Regularly review payroll liability reports to monitor your tax obligations and ensure you have sufficient funds for upcoming payments.

By effectively handling payroll liabilities in QuickBooks and consulting your accountant, you can ensure your business remains compliant with tax regulations and avoids penalties.

# CHAPTER EIGHT
# INVENTORY MANAGEMENT

## Setting Up Inventory Items

Adding inventory items in QuickBooks allows you to track your stock levels, manage purchases, and generate reports to analyse your inventory performance.

### *Here's a breakdown of how to set up inventory items in both QuickBooks Online and QuickBooks Desktop:*

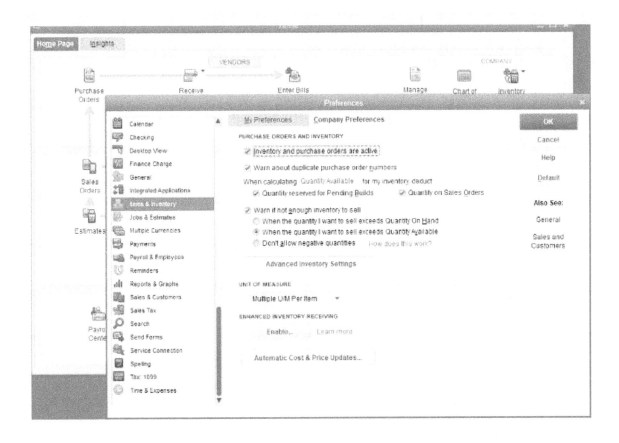

# QuickBooks Online:

1.  **Turn on Inventory Tracking (Optional):** If not already enabled, activate inventory tracking in your settings. This is usually found under **Settings > Sales** or **Items & Inventory**.

2.  **Go to Products and Services:** Navigate to the **Products and Services** section. You might see an **Add New** button or a similar option to create a new item.

3.  **Select Inventory:** Choose **Inventory** as the item type when creating a new product or service.

4.  **Enter Item Details:** Fill in the following details about your inventory item:

    o   **Name:** Enter a clear and descriptive name for your product.

    o   **Description (Optional):** Provide a brief description of the product, especially if relevant for sales or customer orders.

    o   **SKU or Item Number:** Assign a unique identifier for your inventory item (optional but recommended for easier tracking).

    o   **Category:** Categorize your product to group similar items (e.g., clothing, electronics).

    o   **Purchase Cost:** Enter the cost you pay to purchase the item from your vendor.

    o   **Sales Price:** Set the price at which you sell the item to your customers.

    o   **Sales Description (Optional):** A customer-facing description of the product displayed on invoices or sales receipts.

    o   **Tax Information:** Specify any sales tax applicable to the product.

    o   **Inventory Account:** Select the appropriate inventory account from your chart of accounts (usually an asset account like "Inventory").

    o   **Preferred Vendor (Optional):** Indicate your preferred vendor for this product if you have one.

    o   **Reorder Point (Optional):** Set a reorder point to receive automatic alerts when your stock level falls below this threshold.

5.  **Save the Item:** Click **Save** to add the new inventory item to QuickBooks Online.

## QuickBooks Desktop:

1. **Go to the Items Menu:** Click on the **Items** menu within QuickBooks Desktop.

2. **New Item:** Select **New Item** from the menu options.

3. **Item Type:** Choose **Inventory Item** as the item type.

4. **Enter Item Details:** Similar to QuickBooks Online, fill in the details about your inventory item, including name, description, SKU, category, purchase cost, sales price, sales description, tax information, etc.

5. **Inventory Information:** In the inventory information section, you might see additional options like:

   o **Asset Account:** Select the inventory asset account.

   o **Income Account:** Choose the sales income account for this item.

   o **Expense Account:** Specify the expense account for purchases of this item (usually cost of goods sold).

   o **Average Cost Method (Optional):** Select your preferred method for calculating inventory cost (average cost, FIFO, etc.).

6. **Save the Item:** Click **Save** to add the new inventory item to QuickBooks Desktop.

## Additional Tips:

- **Use Clear Descriptions:** Provide clear and informative descriptions for your inventory items to ease identification and sales order accuracy.

- **Inventory Images (Optional):** If using QuickBooks Online Plus or Advanced, you can add images to your inventory items.

- **Inventory Organization:** Utilize categories and subcategories to effectively organize your inventory list for better manageability.

By following these steps and best practices, you can set up inventory items effectively in QuickBooks, ensuring accurate stock tracking and improved inventory management for your business. Remember to consult your accountant if you have any questions regarding inventory accounting practices or specific settings in QuickBooks.

## Tracking Inventory Levels

QuickBooks offers efficient inventory tracking functionalities to help you monitor stock levels, identify low stock situations, and optimize your inventory management.

### *Here's a breakdown of how to track inventory levels in both QuickBooks Online and QuickBooks Desktop:*

## QuickBooks Online:

1. **Enable Inventory Tracking (if not already):** Ensure inventory tracking is activated in your settings. This is usually found under **Settings** > **Sales** or **Items & Inventory**.

2. **Inventory Reports:** Navigate to the **Reports** section and explore reports within the **Inventory** category. Here are some helpful reports for tracking inventory levels:

   - **Inventory Valuation Detail:** This report provides a detailed breakdown of your inventory items, including their quantities, costs, and total value.

   - **Inventory Stock by Item:** This report focuses on the quantity on hand for each inventory item.

   - **Inventory Low Stock Report:** This report identifies inventory items that are falling below your set reorder points, helping you prioritize stock replenishment.

3. **Hover Over Inventory Quantity:** In some inventory or sales reports, you might be able to hover your cursor over the quantity field for an item to see additional details like the average cost and total value of that inventory item.

4. **Inventory Alerts (Optional):** If you've set reorder points for your inventory items, QuickBooks Online can send you notifications when stock levels fall below that threshold. This helps you stay proactive about restocking before you run out.

## QuickBooks Desktop:

1. **Inventory Centre (Optional):** If you have QuickBooks Desktop Premier or Enterprise, you'll have access to the Inventory Centre. This dashboard provides a centralized view of your inventory levels, reorder points, and average sales.

2. **Inventory Reports:** Similar to Online, access reports within the **Inventory** section. Look for reports like:

   o **Inventory Valuation Summary:** This report offers a summary of the total value of your inventory.

   o **Inventory Stock by Item:** This report showcases the on-hand quantity for each inventory item.

   o **Inventory Low Stock Report:** This report identifies items reaching reorder points.

3. **Item List:** The **Item List** within the **Items** menu displays your inventory items. You can see the quantity on hand for each item directly in this list.

By effectively using these features in QuickBooks, you can gain valuable insights into your inventory levels, avoid stockouts, and optimize your inventory management practices for better business efficiency. Remember, consulting your accountant is recommended for any specific inventory tracking questions or inventory management strategies.

## Adjusting Inventory Quantities

QuickBooks Desktop updates inventory quantities and values as you track purchases and sales. However, you may need to record adjustments occasionally to maintain accurate inventory status.

If you're unsure how to do this, don't worry. We'll guide you through identifying the type of adjustment needed and how to create it.

**Note:** If you need to adjust your stock of finished goods, follow this method unless you need to return an assembly's parts to your inventory. For "unbuilding" an assembly item and returning its components to inventory, here's what you can do.

**Step 1: Determine the Type of Adjustment You Need**

**Adjust Quantity on Hand**

- Adjusting product quantity helps track any increases or decreases not due to sales or purchases. This might be necessary for reasons such as item breakage or discrepancies discovered during an inventory count.

**Adjust Total Value**

- The total value of your product is its average cost multiplied by the quantity in stock. Factors like seasonal demand or spoilage can affect this value.

**Tip:** Consult your accountant before adjusting inventory value. If you don't have an accountant, we can help you find one near you.

**Step 2: Set Up Your Inventory Adjustment Account**

Create a separate account in your chart of accounts to track adjustments.

1. Select **Company** and then **Chart of Accounts**.

2. Select the **Account ▼** dropdown, then **New**.

3. From the **Other Account Types ▼** dropdown, select **Cost of Goods Sold**.

4. Name this account "Inventory Adjustments", and then **Save and Close**.

**Step 3: Adjust Your Inventory**

Once you set up your adjustment account, you can adjust a product's quantity, value, or both. Here's how:

1. Select **Vendors** and then **Inventory Activities**.

2. Select **Adjust Quantity/Value on Hand**.

3. Select **Inventory** and then **Adjust Quantity/Value on Hand**.

4. From the **Adjustment Type ▼** dropdown, select **Quantity, Total Value**, or **Quantity and Total Value**. Choose the adjustment type and then select your adjustment account.

5. Enter the **Adjustment Date**.

6. From the **Adjust Account ▼** dropdown, select the adjustment account you set up.

7. Add a **Reference No.** You can also assign a customer, job, or class.

8. Select **Find & Select Items**. Choose the items you want to adjust. Use the **Find** field if you have many items.

9. Select **Add Selected items**.

10. Enter a new quantity or new value (or both) for each item.

**Tip:** When recording a quantity adjustment, check the quantity difference. It should be negative for a decrease in quantity and positive for an increase.

11. Select **Save and Close**.

**Step 4: Verify Your Inventory Status**

Check your inventory status reports to ensure accuracy.

1. Select **Reports** and then **Inventory**.

2. To check your product's value, select the **Inventory Valuation Summary**.

3. To check your product's quantity, select the **Inventory Stock Status by Item**.

4. Look for the items you adjusted and ensure everything is correct.


# Creating Purchase Orders for Inventory

Purchase orders help you communicate with vendors about what you need to order and track those orders to manage upcoming expenses. Here's how to create and manage purchase orders in QuickBooks Desktop.

**For Windows Users**

**Turn on Purchase Orders:**

1. Go to **Edit** and select **Preferences**.

2. Select **Items & Inventory**, then go to the **Company Preferences** tab.

3. Check the **Inventory and purchase orders are active** checkbox and select **OK**.

**Create a Purchase Order:**

1. Go to **Vendors** and select **Create Purchase Orders**.

2. In the **Vendor** dropdown, select the vendor you want to create a purchase order for. You can also select **Add New** to add a new vendor.

3. Fill out the fields and add the items you want to order.

4. Select **Save & Close**.

**Tip:** Purchase orders are part of the Accounts Payable (A/P) workflow. Learn more about the A/P workflow in QuickBooks Desktop.

**For Mac Users**

**Turn on Inventory and Purchase Orders:**

1. Go to the **QuickBooks** menu and select **Preferences**.

2. Select **Inventory** to enable inventory and purchase orders.

**Step 1: Create a Purchase Order:**

1. Go to **Vendors**, then select **Create Purchase Orders**.

2. Select **Create Purchase Order....**

3. Fill out the fields, then select **Save**.

**Create a Purchase Order from an Estimate:**

1. From the estimates window, select **Create Purchase Order**.

2. Choose **For all allowed items on the estimate** if the items are from one vendor, or **For selected items...** if there are items from multiple vendors. Then select the items you want on your purchase order.

3. Select **OK**.

4. Fill out the fields, then select **Save**.

**Step 2: Track Your Open Purchase Orders**

**View All Open Purchase Orders:**

1.  Go to the **Lists** menu and select **Customer & Vendor Profiles**, then **Purchase Orders**.

2.  Change the **View:** filter from **All Purchase Orders** to **Open Purchase Orders**.

3.  To see the history of the orders, select the **History** icon in the Purchase Orders window.

**List Open Purchase Orders for a Specific Item:**

1.  Go to **Lists**, then select **Items**.

2.  Select the item, then choose **QuickReport** from the ⚙▼ dropdown menu.

3.  Double-click a purchase order to view details.

**Create a Report of Your Open Purchase Orders:**

1.  Go to **Reports** and select **Purchases**.

2.  Select **Open Purchase Orders**.

3.  To print the report, select the **Print** icon.

**Edit a Purchase Order:**

1.  Go to **Vendors**, then select **Purchase Order List**.

2.  Double-click the vendor with the purchase order you want to edit. The purchase orders window appears.

3.  Select the purchase order you want to edit. If you don't see the purchase order list, select the **Left View** icon.

**Step 3: Record the Items You Received**

When you receive goods ordered with a purchase order, record it in QuickBooks. The transaction type depends on when you pay for the items:

- **Create an item receipt** if you'll get the bill later.

- **Create a bill** if you received a bill when you received the items.

- **Create a check or credit card charge** if you paid for the items immediately.

94

For inventory items, record the items you received. QuickBooks will mark the purchase order as **Received in Full** once all items are received. If you don't expect to receive all items, you can manually close the purchase order.

## Receiving Inventory

There are two main scenarios for receiving inventory in QuickBooks:

1. **Receiving inventory you've already ordered:** This applies when you create a purchase order for the inventory items and the vendor sends them later.

2. **Receiving inventory without a purchase order:** This might be the case for unexpected deliveries or situations where you haven't placed a formal purchase order beforehand.

Here's a breakdown of how to handle both scenarios in QuickBooks Online and QuickBooks Desktop:

**QuickBooks Online:**

**Receiving with Purchase Order:**

1. Go to the + **New** menu and under **Vendor** select **Bill**.

2. Choose the vendor you received the inventory from.

3. QuickBooks will display a list of open purchase orders for that vendor (if any). Select the relevant purchase order to associate the received inventory with the existing order.

4. Review the information on the bill. You can edit quantities or adjust item details if needed.

5. Click **Save and close** to record the receipt of inventory and update your inventory stock levels.

**Receiving without Purchase Order:**

1. Go to the + **New** menu and select **Inventory quantity adjustment**.

2. Enter the adjustment date.

3. Select the inventory items you received and enter the quantities.

4. Click **Save and close** to update your inventory stock levels.

**QuickBooks Desktop:**

**Receiving with Purchase Order:**

1. Go to the **Receive Inventory** dropdown menu and select **Receive Inventory with Bill**.

2. From the **Supplier** dropdown, choose the vendor that sent the inventory.

3. Select **Yes** to receive against a purchase order.

4. Choose the correct purchase order from the list.

5. Review the information on the bill. You can edit quantities or adjust item details if needed.

6. Click **Save & Close** to record the receipt of inventory and update your inventory stock levels.

**Receiving without Purchase Order:**

1. Go to the **Receive Inventory** dropdown menu and select **Receive Inventory without bill**.

2. From the dropdown, choose the vendor name (or select **<No Vendor>** if applicable).

3. Select **Yes** to receive against a purchase order (choose **No** if there's no purchase order).

4. If applicable, choose the correct purchase order from the list.

5. Review the information on the item receipt. You can edit quantities or adjust item details if needed.

6. Click **Save & Close** to update your inventory stock levels.

**Important Notes:**

- **Matching Items:** Ensure you're selecting the correct inventory items when recording their receipt.

- **Quantity Adjustments:** If the received quantities differ from what you ordered (or expected), adjust the quantities accordingly in QuickBooks.

- **Bill Payments:** When receiving with a purchase order, you'll typically record the bill payment at a later date.

By understanding these methods, you can effectively record inventory received in QuickBooks, maintaining accurate stock levels and ensuring proper tracking of your inventory. Remember to consult your accountant for any specific inventory management practices or questions you might have.

# CHAPTER NINE
# REPORTING

## Running Standard Report

Running standard reports in QuickBooks is a straightforward process that allows you to access pre-built reports covering various aspects of your business finances. Here's a breakdown of how to run standard reports in both QuickBooks Online and QuickBooks Desktop:

**QuickBooks Online:**

1. **Access the Reports Menu:** Navigate to the **Reports** section within QuickBooks Online. This might be displayed as a menu option or a dedicated tab depending on your version.

2. **Browse or Search for Reports:** QuickBooks Online offers a variety of standard reports categorized by type (e.g., Sales and Customers, Expenses and Vendors, etc.). You can browse through the report categories or use the search bar to find a specific report by name.

3. **Select the Report:** Click on the desired report to open it.

4. **View or Print (Optional):** The report will display the data in a formatted view. You can review the report on-screen or utilize the print option to generate a physical copy.

5. **Customize (Optional):** Most standard reports in QuickBooks Online allow you to customize them further. Look for the **Edit** or **Customize** button (might vary depending on the report). This allows you to:

   o **Date Range:** Specify the timeframe for the data you want to see in the report.

   o **Filters:** Apply filters to narrow down the report data based on specific criteria (e.g., customer, vendor, class).

   o **Columns:** Add, remove, or reorder columns to display the data points most relevant to your needs.

**QuickBooks Desktop:**

1. **Go to the Reports Menu:** Click on the **Reports** menu within QuickBooks Desktop.

2. **Standard Reports List:** A list of available standard reports will be displayed, categorized by type.

3. **Select the Report:** Choose the report you want to run by clicking on its name.

4. **View or Print (Optional):** Similar to QuickBooks Online, the report will be displayed on-screen. You can review it or utilize the print option for a hard copy.

5. **Customize (Optional):** QuickBooks Desktop also allows customizing standard reports. Click on the **Customize Report** button to modify:

    o **Dates:** Specify the date range for the report data.

    o **Filters:** Apply filters to narrow down the data based on various criteria.

    o **Levels:** (For certain reports) Choose how you want to group or sort the data (e.g., by customer, by class).

    o **Display Options:** Select which data columns to display in the report.

    o **Sorting:** Define how you want to sort the report rows.

**Additional Tips:**

- **Report Gallery:** Both QuickBooks Online and Desktop offer report galleries with a wide range of pre-defined reports. Explore these galleries to discover reports relevant to your needs.

- **Memorize Reports:** Save your customized reports as memorized reports for easy access in the future (refer to [PROMPT 9.1 Memorizing Reports]('#PROMPT 9.1 Memorizing Reports') for details).

By following these steps, you can efficiently run standard reports in QuickBooks, gaining valuable insights into your business finances. Remember, even with standard reports, consider customizing them to focus on the data most relevant to your needs and make informed financial decisions.

## Customizing Reports

QuickBooks offers a robust reporting system that you can customize to fit your specific needs. Here's a breakdown of how to customize reports in both QuickBooks Online and QuickBooks Desktop:

**QuickBooks Online:**

There are two main approaches to report customization in QuickBooks Online:

**1. Modifying Standard Reports:**

- Access the report you want to customize from the **Reports** menu.

- Look for the **Edit** or **Customize** option (might vary depending on the report).

- This will allow you to:

    o **Date Range:** Specify the timeframe for the data you want to see in the report.

    o **Filters:** Apply filters to narrow down the report data based on specific criteria (e.g., customer, vendor, class).

    o **Columns:** Add, remove, or reorder columns to display the data points most relevant to your needs.

    o **Rows:** In some reports, you can group or sort rows by different criteria to analyse trends or patterns.

- Once you've made your customizations, save the report for future use.

**2. Creating Custom Reports:**

- In some versions of QuickBooks Online, you can create reports entirely from scratch.

- This allows you to select the specific data fields you want to include and customize the report layout to your needs.

**QuickBooks Desktop:**

- Customizing reports in QuickBooks Desktop involves a similar process:

**Steps:**

1. Open the report you want to customize from the **Reports** menu.

2. Click on the **Customize Report** button.

3. This opens the **Modify Report** window, where you can:

    ▪ **Dates:** Specify the date range for the report data.

- **Filters:** Apply filters to narrow down the data based on various criteria.

- **Levels:** (For certain reports) Choose how you want to group or sort the data (e.g., by customer, by class).

- **Display Options:** Select which data columns to display in the report.

- **Sorting:** Define how you want to sort the report rows.

- Once you've made your customizations, you can save the report template for future use.

**Additional Tips:**

- **Report Gallery:** Both QuickBooks Online and Desktop offer report galleries with a wide range of pre-defined reports. Explore these galleries to find reports relevant to your needs and customize them further if necessary.

- **Memorize Reports:** Save your customized reports as memorized reports for easy access in the future.

- **Consult Your Accountant:** Complex reports or those with tax implications might require guidance from your accountant to ensure you're customizing them appropriately.

By understanding these customization options, you can leverage the power of reporting in QuickBooks to gain valuable insights into your business finances. Tailoring reports to your specific needs allows you to track key metrics, identify trends, and make informed business decisions.

## Memorizing Reports

In QuickBooks, memorizing reports allows you to save your customized reports for quick and easy access in the future. This saves you time from repeatedly customizing reports with the same filters, dates, and settings. Here's a breakdown of memorizing reports in both QuickBooks Online and QuickBooks Desktop:

**QuickBooks Online:**

1. **Generate and Customize Your Report:** Access the desired report from the **Reports** menu in QuickBooks Online. Apply any necessary filters, date ranges, or other customizations to tailor the report to your needs.

2. **Memorize the Report:** Once you're satisfied with the report's presentation, locate the **Memorize** or **Save as Custom** option (depending on your version). This option might be displayed as a menu button or icon within the report view.

3. **Enter a Memo Name:** Provide a descriptive name for your memorized report to easily identify it later. Choose a name that reflects the report's purpose or the specific customizations you applied.

4. **Save the Memorized Report:** Click **Save** or **OK** to finalize the memorization process. Your customized report will now be available for quick access.

**QuickBooks Desktop:**

1. **Customize Your Report:** Open the report you want to memorize from the **Reports** menu in QuickBooks Desktop. Utilize the **Customize Report** button to modify dates, filters, and other settings as needed.

2. **Access Memorize Report Option:** Locate the **Memorize Report** button within the report window (it might be under the **Edit** menu).

3. **Enter a Memo Name:** Similar to QuickBooks Online, provide a clear and descriptive name for your memorized report for easy identification.

4. **Save the Memorized Report:** Click **Save** or **OK** to complete the memorization process. Your customized report will be accessible for future use.

**Accessing Memorized Reports:**

- **QuickBooks Online:** Look for the **Memorized Reports** section within the **Reports** menu. You'll find your saved reports listed there for easy access.

- **QuickBooks Desktop:** Go to the **Reports** menu and select **Memorized Reports**. Your saved reports will be displayed in a list for you to choose from.

**Benefits of Memorizing Reports:**

- **Saves Time:** Avoids the need to repeatedly customize reports with the same settings.

- **Improved Efficiency:** Provides quick access to frequently used reports, streamlining your workflow.

- **Consistency:** Ensures you're always viewing reports with the same customizations for accurate comparisons over time.

By memorizing reports in QuickBooks, you can significantly enhance your reporting efficiency and gain faster insights into your business data. Remember to consult your accountant if you have any questions regarding specific report customizations or data analysis needs.

## Exporting Reports to Excel

Exporting reports to Excel allows you to further analyse and manipulate your QuickBooks data in a familiar spreadsheet format. Here's a breakdown of exporting reports to Excel in both QuickBooks Online and QuickBooks Desktop:

**QuickBooks Online:**

1. **Generate Your Report:** Access the desired report from the **Reports** menu in QuickBooks Online.

2. **Export to Excel:** Locate the **Export** button or icon within the report view. This might be located in a menu or toolbar.

3. **Choose Export Format:** Select **Export to Excel** from the available export options.

4. **Save or Download:** QuickBooks Online might prompt you to choose a location to save the Excel file or initiate the download directly.

**QuickBooks Desktop:**

1. **Open Your Report:** Navigate to the **Reports** menu in QuickBooks Desktop and select the report you want to export.

2. **Export to Excel:** Click on the **Excel** button or dropdown within the report window (it might be located on the toolbar).

3. **Export Options (Optional):** In some versions of QuickBooks Desktop, you might be presented with additional options:

   o **Create New Worksheet:** This creates a new Excel file with your report data.

o **Update Existing Worksheet:** This allows you to update an existing Excel file with the report data (useful for maintaining historical data). Make sure to choose the correct file and be cautious not to overwrite existing data unintentionally.

4. **Save or Export:** Click **OK** or **Save** to finalize the export process. Your report data will be exported to a new or existing Excel file.

**Important Notes:**

- **Formatting and Layouts:** Exported reports might not retain the exact formatting or layout from QuickBooks. You might need to adjust the formatting within Excel for better presentation.

- **Data Limitations:** There might be limitations on the amount of data you can export to Excel in a single report.

- **Charts and Graphs:** Exported data might not include charts or graphs that were present in the original QuickBooks report. You can recreate these visuals in Excel if needed.

**Additional Tips:**

- **Excel Skills:** Having some familiarity with Excel will help you effectively manipulate and analyse the exported data.

- **PivotTables and Charts:** Utilize Excel's features like pivot tables and charts to gain deeper insights from your exported reports.

- **Data Security:** Ensure you export reports containing sensitive financial data to a secure location.

By understanding these steps and considerations, you can effectively export reports from QuickBooks to Excel, gaining the flexibility to analyse your business data in a spreadsheet format and leverage Excel's functionalities for further exploration.

# Sharing Reports

Sharing reports in QuickBooks allows you to collaborate with colleagues, accountants, or external stakeholders by providing them access to your financial data. Here's a breakdown of sharing reports in both QuickBooks Online and QuickBooks Desktop:

**QuickBooks Online:**

QuickBooks Online offers a more comprehensive approach to sharing reports, with varying levels of access control:

**Sharing with Email:**

1. **Generate Your Report:** Access the report you want to share from the **Reports** menu.

2. **Share Option:** Locate the **Share** button or icon within the report view.

3. **Enter Email Addresses:** Add the email addresses of the people you want to share the report with.

4. **Access Level:** Choose the access level you want to grant (e.g., view only, edit, or collaborate).

5. **Delivery Options (Optional):** Depending on your version, you might have options to set an expiration date for access or include a personalized message.

6. **Send:** Click **Send** to share the report via email.

**Sharing with Accountant (optional):**

QuickBooks Online offers secure accountant access features. Consult your accountant for details on setting this up, allowing them to access and collaborate on your reports directly within QuickBooks Online.

**QuickBooks Desktop:**

Sharing reports in QuickBooks Desktop is more limited:

1. **Export the Report:** Export the report you want to share to Excel using the methods mentioned previously in [PROMPT 9.1 Exporting Reports to Excel](#PROMPT 9.1 Exporting Reports to Excel).

2. **Share the Exported File:** Share the exported Excel file using your preferred method (email, file sharing services, etc.).

**Important Considerations:**

- **Security:** Be mindful of the access level you grant when sharing reports, especially those containing sensitive financial data.

- **Data Accuracy:** Ensure the report you're sharing reflects the most up-to-date and accurate information.

- **Context (Optional):** Consider including a brief explanation or context for the report, especially if sharing with someone unfamiliar with your business.

**Additional Tips:**

- **Collaboration Tools:** For more advanced collaboration needs, consider using cloud-based collaboration tools where you can share and discuss reports with your team in real-time.

- **Password Protection (Optional):** If sharing the report via file sharing services, you might consider adding password protection for an extra layer of security.

By understanding the sharing options in QuickBooks and considering these important points, you can effectively share reports with relevant individuals while maintaining data security and fostering collaboration around your business finances. Remember to consult your accountant for guidance on sharing reports with them or for any specific security concerns you might have.

# CHAPTER TEN
# YEAR-END TASK

## Preparing for Year-End

Closing the books at the end of the year is an essential chore for any firm that uses QuickBooks Desktop. This desktop-enabled program guarantees that your financial records are accurate and up to date, and it helps you prepare for tax season.

**Step 1: Review and Reconcile Your Accounts for Year-End in QuickBooks**

Before diving into year-end procedures in QuickBooks, a thorough review and reconciliation of your accounts is essential. This ensures all your financial transactions are accurate and accounted for, laying a solid foundation for closing the books. Here's what to focus on:

**Reconciling Bank and Credit Card Accounts:**

- **Match Transactions:** Carefully compare your bank and credit card statements to the corresponding transactions recorded in QuickBooks. This ensures all deposits, withdrawals, fees, and other activities are accurately reflected in your system.

- **Identify Discrepancies:** If you find any mismatches, investigate the cause. This could involve uncleared checks, deposits in transit, or errors in data entry. Resolve these discrepancies before proceeding.

**Reviewing and Adjusting Outstanding Transactions:**

- **Identify Outstanding Items:** Look for transactions marked as "outstanding" or "pending." These might include unpaid invoices, uncashed checks, or bills awaiting payment.

- **Ensure Proper Accounting:** Verify that these outstanding transactions are categorized correctly and accurately reflect your current financial position.

- **Make Adjustments:** If necessary, adjust the outstanding transactions. This could involve recording payments received, voiding uncashed checks, or updating invoice statuses.

**Resolving Discrepancies:**

- **Identify Errors:** Meticulously examine your financial records for any inconsistencies or errors. This might include incorrect amounts, typos in account names, or duplicate entries.

- **Resolve Issues:** Take corrective actions to address identified discrepancies. This could involve correcting data entry mistakes, adjusting account balances, or reconciling differences between your records and bank statements.

By following these steps, you can ensure your QuickBooks data is accurate and ready for year-end closing procedures. Remember, clean and reconciled accounts lead to reliable financial reports and a smoother year-end experience.

**Step 2: Safeguard Your Data with a Backup Before Year-End Close**

Before embarking on QuickBooks year-end procedures, creating a reliable backup of your data is crucial. This safeguard ensures you can restore your financial information if any unforeseen issues arise during the closing process. Here's how to back up your data and some additional considerations:

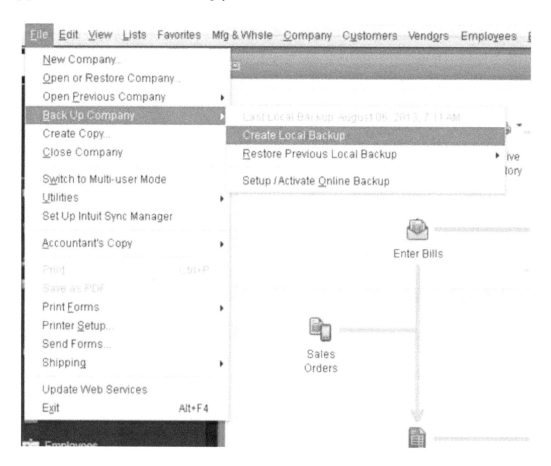

**Creating a Backup:**

1. Go to the **File** menu in QuickBooks Online.

2. Select **Back Up Company**.

3. Choose a secure location to save your backup file. This could be an external hard drive, a cloud storage service, or both for added security.

4. Click **Save** to create the backup.

**Backup Considerations:**

- **Secure Location:** Select a location with robust security measures to protect your sensitive financial data. External hard drives or reputable cloud storage services are ideal options.

- **Testing the Backup:** It's wise to verify the functionality of your backup. Close QuickBooks Online and attempt to restore the backup file. If you can successfully access the restored data, your backup is functional.

- **Multiple Copies:** Having multiple copies of your backup file in different locations is highly recommended. This protects you in case of data loss due to hardware failure or other unforeseen circumstances. Consider both an external hard drive and cloud storage for redundancy.

By following these steps and keeping your data secure, you can approach QuickBooks year-end closing with peace of mind, knowing you have a reliable backup in case of any mishaps.

**Step 3: Understanding Year-End Closing in QuickBooks**

Year-End Closing in QuickBooks involves finalizing your financial records for the past year and preparing your data for the new year. Here's a breakdown of the process for both QuickBooks Desktop and QuickBooks Online:

**QuickBooks Desktop:**

- **Manual Adjustments:** Unlike Online, Desktop doesn't have an automated closing function. You'll need to make manual year-end adjustments through journal entries. These adjustments might include:

o   Accruing expenses (e.g., salaries owed but not yet paid).

o   Recording prepaid expenses (e.g., unused portion of insurance).

o   Adjusting inventory levels based on physical counts.

- **Review and Verification:** Before creating journal entries, carefully analyse your income statement, balance sheet, and cash flow statement to identify necessary adjustments.

- **Creating Journal Entries:** Once adjustments are identified, use the Journal Entry function to record them in QuickBooks. These entries typically close income and expense accounts, transferring their net income or loss to a retained earnings account.

- **Update Fiscal Year:** Finally, update your fiscal year to reflect the new year. You can do this by going to **Edit** > **Preferences** > **Company Preferences** and setting the new closing date under **Closing date**.

| Closing Entry | | | |
|---|---|---|---|
| Date | Account Name | Debit | Credit |
| December 31 | | | |
| | Income Summary | 14,850.00 | |
| | -Cost of Goods Sold | | 10,200.00 |
| | -Depreciation Expense | | 2,000.00 |
| | -Rent Expense | | 500.00 |
| | -Supplies Expense | | 500.00 |
| | -Utilities Expense | | 400.00 |
| | -Wages Expense | | 750.00 |
| | -Interest Expense | | 500.00 |
| | Close Expense Accounts to Income Summary | | |

**QuickBooks Online:**

- **Simplified Closing:** QuickBooks Online offers a more streamlined year-end closing process.

- **Enable Close the Books:** Go to **Settings** (gear icon) and select **Accounts and settings**. In the **Advanced** tab, activate the **Close the books** switch.

- **Set Closing Date:** Choose a suitable date to mark the end of your fiscal year. This restricts future edits to transactions before that date.

- **Optional: Closing Date Password:** For enhanced security, you can set a password to limit access to past year-end data.

**Important Notes:**

- Regardless of the platform (Desktop or Online), consulting with your accountant before year-end closing is highly recommended. They can advise you on specific adjustments relevant to your business and tax situation.

- While QuickBooks Online offers "Close the books," it doesn't necessarily close accounts in the traditional accounting sense. It primarily restricts edits to past transactions and prepares your file for the new year. You might still need to make manual adjustments based on your financial situation.

By understanding these steps and the key differences between Desktop and Online, you can effectively navigate year-end closing in QuickBooks and ensure your financial records are accurate for the new year.

**Step 4: Verify and Finalize Your Year-End Closing Entries in QuickBooks**

After specifying how each account will be handled (closed or carried over), QuickBooks takes care of generating a report detailing the closing entries that will impact your financial statements. This step involves meticulously reviewing the report for accuracy before finalizing the year-end closing process.

**Reviewing the Closing Entries Report:**

- **Scrutinize Each Entry:** Carefully examine each closing entry in the report, ensuring they align with your understanding and financial statements. Pay close attention to entries affecting:

    - **Annual Profit or Loss Report (Balance Sheet):** This report summarizes your company's financial health at a specific point, usually the fiscal year-end. It reflects your assets (cash, inventory, property), liabilities (loans, debts), and equity (difference between assets and liabilities).

- o **Income Statement:** This statement details your business's financial activity over a period, typically a year. It reveals your revenue, expenses, and net income (profit) or loss.

- o **Cash Flow Statement:** This statement tracks the movement of cash in and out of your business during a specific timeframe. It includes details about cash inflows (sales, loans) and outflows (expenses, investments).

- **Identify Discrepancies:** If you find any inconsistencies with your expectations, investigate the cause. This might involve consulting your adjustments or recalculating figures.

| Accounts | Debits | Credits |
|---|---|---|
| Cash | $41,150 | |
| Accounts Receivable | 4,806 | |
| Allowance for Doubtful Accounts | | 58 |
| Inventory | 2,670 | |
| Prepaid Insurance | 2,200 | |
| Land | 20,000 | |
| Accounts Payable | | 1,500 |
| Interest Payable | | 90 |
| Payroll Taxes Payable | | 113 |
| Wages Payable | | 817 |
| Mortgage Payable | | 18,000 |
| Owner's Investment | | 50,000 |
| Retained Earnings | | - |
| Sales | | 11,680 |
| Repair Revenue | | 20 |
| Cost of Goods Sold | 3,504 | |
| Advertising | 200 | |
| Bad Debt Expense | 58 | |
| Bank Charges | 50 | |
| Insurance Expense | 200 | |
| Payroll Taxes | 603 | |
| Rent | 2,240 | |
| Supplies | 150 | |
| Wages | 4,357 | |
| Interest Expense | 90 | |
| | $82,278 | $82,278 |

**Making Adjustments (if necessary):**

- **Refine Closing Entries:** If you discover discrepancies, you can return to the "Chart of Accounts" and modify the closing entries for specific accounts. This ensures the generated report accurately reflects your financial situation.

**Finalizing Year-End Closing:**

- **Once you're confident in the accuracy of the closing entries, you can proceed with finalizing the year-end closing process in QuickBooks.**

**Additional Tips:**

- Consult your accountant throughout the year-end closing process. They can provide invaluable guidance on adjustments, entries, and ensuring compliance with accounting standards.

- Maintain clear records of your year-end closing procedures. This documentation serves as a reference point for future reference or audits.

By meticulously reviewing and verifying your year-end closing entries in QuickBooks, you can ensure the accuracy of your financial statements and gain valuable insights into your business performance.

**Step 5: Finalize Year-End Closing in QuickBooks Online**

Once you've meticulously reviewed and verified your closing entries in the generated report (Step 4), you're ready to finalize the year-end closing process in QuickBooks Online. Here's what to do:

- **Confidence in Accuracy:** Double-check that all closing entries are accurate and align with your expectations.

- **Finalize Closing (Optional):** While QuickBooks Online doesn't require a finalization step like Desktop, you can leverage the "Close the books" feature for an extra layer of control. This restricts edits to transactions from the prior year.

**Important Note:** Consulting your accountant throughout the year-end closing process is highly recommended. They can advise on specific adjustments and ensure your entries comply with accounting standards.

**Step 6: Update Your QuickBooks File for the New Year**

Now that you've finalized your year-end closing (or reviewed entries in Desktop), it's time to prepare your QuickBooks file for the new year:

1. **Go to Settings:** Access the Settings menu in QuickBooks Online (gear icon).

2. **Update Fiscal Year:** Locate the "Company Preferences" or "Account Settings" section (depending on your version). Find the "Fiscal Year" setting and update it to reflect the new year.

3. **Save Changes:** Click "Save" or confirm the update to ensure your QuickBooks file is ready for the upcoming year.

By following these steps, you'll successfully finalize your year-end closing and update your QuickBooks data for the new year. Remember, consulting your accountant can provide valuable guidance throughout the process.

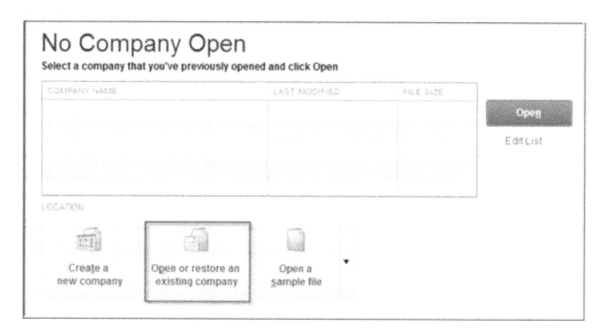

By following these steps, you've effectively completed the year-end closing process in QuickBooks. This ensures your financial records are accurate and prepared for the new year.

**Important Note:**

For a more comprehensive year-end strategy and to ensure compliance with accounting standards, consulting with your accountant is highly recommended. They can provide invaluable guidance throughout the process.

# Generating Year-End Reports

Year-end is a crucial time to analyse your business performance and financial health. QuickBooks Online offers a robust selection of reports to help you gain valuable insights through this process. Here's a breakdown of some key reports to consider generating at year-end:

**Profit and Loss Report:**

- This report summarizes your business's income and expenses over a specific period, typically a year.

- Analyse your revenue streams, identify your cost drivers, and calculate your net income (profit) or loss.

- Use this report to compare your performance to previous years or industry benchmarks.

**Balance Sheet:**

- This report provides a snapshot of your company's financial position at a specific point in time, usually the end of the fiscal year.

- It categorizes your assets (what you own), liabilities (what you owe), and equity (the difference between assets and liabilities).

- Use the balance sheet to assess your financial stability and track changes in your assets and liabilities over time.

**Cash Flow Statement:**

- This report details the movement of cash into and out of your business during a specific period.

- It categorizes your cash inflows (from sales, loans) and outflows (for expenses, investments).

- Use the cash flow statement to understand your cash flow situation, identify potential cash flow gaps, and make informed financial decisions.

**Accounts Receivable Aging Summary:**

- This report provides a breakdown of your outstanding customer invoices by age category (e.g., current, 30-60 days past due, over 90 days past due).

- Use this report to identify overdue invoices, prioritize collections efforts, and improve your cash flow.

**Accounts Payable Aging Summary:**

- This report details your outstanding bills from vendors by age category.

- Use this report to manage your liabilities effectively, prioritize payments to vendors, and ensure timely bill settlements.

**Inventory Valuation Summary:**

- (If you manage inventory) This report summarizes the value of your on-hand inventory at a specific date.

- It can help you identify potential inventory discrepancies, optimize your inventory levels, and reduce carrying costs.

**Additional Tips:**

- Customize report parameters like date ranges or specific accounts for a more focused analysis.

- Export reports to spreadsheets or other applications for further analysis or sharing with your accountant.

- Compare year-end reports to previous periods to track trends and measure your business growth.

By generating and analysing these year-end reports in QuickBooks Online, you can gain valuable insights into your financial performance, identify areas for improvement, and make informed business decisions for the upcoming year.

# Closing the Books

Year-end closing in QuickBooks Online involves finalizing your financial records for the past year and preparing your data for the new year. While the process is simpler than traditional accounting methods, it's still an important step to ensure accurate financial reporting. Here's a breakdown of the key steps for closing the books in QuickBooks Online:

**1. Review and Reconcile Accounts:**

- Before closing the books, ensure all your financial transactions are accurate and accounted for.

- Reconcile your bank and credit card statements with your QuickBooks records to identify and resolve any discrepancies.

- Review outstanding invoices and bills to ensure they are categorized correctly.

## 2. Back Up Your Data:

- Creating a reliable backup of your QuickBooks Online data is crucial before any year-end procedures.

- This safeguard allows you to restore your financial information if any unforeseen issues arise during closing.

- Back up your data to a secure location like an external hard drive or a cloud storage service.

## 3. Close the Books (Optional):

- QuickBooks Online offers a simplified "Close the books" function:

  - Go to **Settings** (gear icon) and select **Accounts and settings**.

  - In the **Advanced** tab, activate the **Close the books** switch.

- This feature restricts edits to transactions from the previous year, but it doesn't necessarily close accounts in the traditional accounting sense.

- You might still need to make manual adjustments based on your financial situation (refer to your accountant for guidance).

## 4. Set Closing Date:

- Choose a convenient date to mark the end of your fiscal year. This restricts edits to transactions before that date.

## 5. Optional: Closing Date Password:

- For enhanced security, you can set a password to limit access to past year-end data.

## 6. Generate Year-End Reports:

- After closing the books (or reviewing entries), generate essential year-end reports like Profit and Loss, Balance Sheet, Cash Flow Statement, and Accounts Receivable/Payable Aging Summaries.

- Analyse these reports to gain valuable insights into your business performance, identify areas for improvement, and make informed financial decisions for the upcoming year.

**Important Notes:**

- Consulting with your accountant before year-end closing is highly recommended. They can advise you on specific adjustments relevant to your business and tax situation.

- Remember, "Close the books" in QuickBooks Online primarily restricts edits and prepares your file for the new year. It might not fully replace traditional closing procedures depending on your accounting needs.

By following these steps and consulting your accountant, you can effectively close the books in QuickBooks Online and gain valuable insights for the upcoming year.

# Archiving Your Data

There are two main approaches to archiving data in QuickBooks, depending on whether you're using QuickBooks Online or QuickBooks Desktop:

**QuickBooks Online:**

- **Exporting Data:** QuickBooks Online doesn't offer a traditional archiving function. However, you can export specific data sets you want to preserve for future reference. Here's how:

  1. Go to the **Reports** menu and select the report you want to export (e.g., Profit and Loss, Transactions List).

  2. Click the **Export** icon (usually an arrow pointing downwards).

  3. Choose the desired export format (Excel, CSV, PDF) and select the date range for the data you want to export.

  4. Save the exported file to a secure location on your computer or cloud storage.

- **Long-Term Storage Considerations:** If you need to archive large amounts of data or for an extended period, consider exporting multiple reports or using third-party archiving tools that integrate with QuickBooks Online.

**QuickBooks Desktop:**

- **Condensing Data:** QuickBooks Desktop offers a "Condense Data" utility that helps you archive older data while maintaining core financial information. Here's how to use it:

  1. Go to **File** menu and select **Utilities**.

  2. Choose **Condense Data**.

  3. The tool offers options to:

     - Keep all transactions but remove audit trail information.

     - Keep a specific number of closed periods and remove older data.

  4. Select the appropriate option based on your archiving needs.

  5. Click **OK** to proceed with condensing the data.

**Important Considerations:**

- **Consult Your Accountant:** Before archiving any data, it's wise to consult with your accountant. They can advise on legal and tax regulations regarding data retention for your business.

- **Accessibility:** Ensure you can easily access archived data when needed. Consider using a clear naming system for exported files or archived QuickBooks Desktop files.

- **Security:** Store archived data securely, whether on a physical drive or cloud storage. Implement appropriate security measures to protect sensitive financial information.

By understanding these approaches and considering the important points, you can effectively archive your QuickBooks data and maintain a clean and manageable file for your ongoing accounting needs.

# CHAPTER ELEVEN
# TROUBLESHING AND SUPPORT

## Common Issues and Solutions

QuickBooks Pro Desktop, while powerful, can encounter occasional issues. Here's a breakdown of some common problems and troubleshooting steps you can try:

### 1. Installation or Upgrade Issues:

- **Problem:** Error messages occur during installation or upgrade.

- **Solution:** Ensure your computer meets the system requirements for your desired QuickBooks Pro Desktop version. Check the Intuit website for compatibility information.

- You can also try downloading the installation file again in case of file corruption during download. Rebooting your computer before installation can sometimes resolve conflicts with other programs.

### 2. Running Slow:

- **Problem:** QuickBooks Pro Desktop performance is sluggish, especially in multi-user mode.

- **Solution:** Close any unnecessary programs running in the background. Ensure your computer has sufficient RAM and free disk space to handle QuickBooks Pro Desktop's demands.

- Consider running the QuickBooks File Doctor tool to diagnose and potentially fix data integrity issues within your company file.

### 3. Data File Won't Open or Crashes:

- **Problem:** You encounter errors or crashes when trying to open your company file.

- **Solution:** Verify that your company file isn't already open by another user. Try restarting your computer and then opening the file again.

- Utilize the QuickBooks File Doctor tool to scan and potentially repair your company file. In severe cases, you might need to restore from a backup if available.

### 4. Unable to Print Reports or Forms:

- **Problem:** You're facing issues printing reports or forms from QuickBooks Pro Desktop.

- **Solution:** Ensure your printer is properly connected and powered on. Check if the correct printer is selected within QuickBooks Pro Desktop settings.

- Try updating your printer drivers to ensure compatibility. You can also preview the report or form before printing to identify formatting issues.

**5. Error Messages During Data Entry or Calculations:**

- **Problem:** You encounter error messages when entering data or performing calculations within QuickBooks Pro Desktop.

- **Solution:** Double-check your data entry for any typos or inconsistencies that might trigger errors.

- Verify you're using the correct account types for your transactions. Ensure your company file isn't corrupted by running the QuickBooks File Doctor tool.

By following these steps and utilizing the available resources, you can often resolve common QuickBooks Pro Desktop issues and keep your accounting software running smoothly. It's important to note that if you encounter complex problems beyond your troubleshooting abilities, you might consider seeking assistance from an Intuit certified QuickBooks Pro advisor.

## Using the QuickBooks Help Feature

QuickBooks Pro Desktop offers several ways to access its built-in help features to find answers to your questions and troubleshoot any issues you encounter. Here's a breakdown of the available options:

**1. Help Menu:**

The Help menu is the most straightforward way to access QuickBooks Pro Desktop's built-in help resources. Here's what you can find:

- **Help Topics:** A searchable database containing articles, tutorials, and FAQs on various QuickBooks Pro Desktop functionalities.

- **Search Bar:** Type in keywords related to your issue and the search bar will display relevant help articles and resources within the software.

- **Online Help:** This option might direct you to the Intuit QuickBooks website for more comprehensive online resources.

## 2. Context-Sensitive Help:

QuickBooks Pro Desktop offers context-sensitive help. Right-click on almost any element within the software (menus, buttons, fields) and select "What's This?" A pop-up window will display brief information or instructions related to the specific element you clicked on.

## 3. Help Centre Link:

Within QuickBooks Pro Desktop, you might find a "Help Center" link located somewhere in the user interface (placement might vary depending on the version).

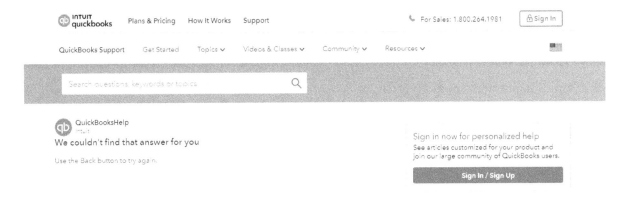

## 4. QuickBooks Online Help (Limited Usefulness):

While it pertains to the cloud-based version, the QuickBooks Online Help Centre might still contain articles and resources relevant to QuickBooks Pro Desktop functionalities, especially for core accounting tasks. However, keep in mind that some features or functionalities might differ between the two versions.

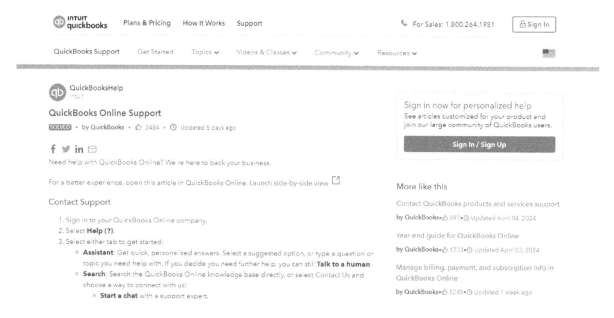

## Additional Tips:

- **Search Options:** Utilize the search bar within the Help menu or the online Help Centre to find specific topics using relevant keywords.

- **Community Resources:** The Intuit QuickBooks website offers a community forum where you can search for solutions or post your questions for help from other QuickBooks users and professionals.

- **Video Tutorials:** Explore the video tutorials available on the Intuit website or YouTube channels to learn about specific QuickBooks Pro Desktop features visually.

By effectively using the built-in help features and exploring online resources, you can find valuable information and guidance to navigate QuickBooks Pro Desktop and address any challenges you encounter while managing your finances.

## Contacting QuickBooks Support

While QuickBooks Pro Desktop offers built-in help features and online resources, there might be situations where you need to contact QuickBooks support directly for further assistance. Here's an overview of the contact options available:

**Phone Support:**

- This is the most direct way to connect with a QuickBooks support representative. However, wait times can vary.

- Look for the phone number on the Intuit QuickBooks website or within your QuickBooks Pro Desktop software (location may vary depending on the version).

- Phone support hours typically operate during weekdays with extended hours on some days. Be prepared with your QuickBooks product information and a description of the issue you're facing.

**Online Chat Support:**

- QuickBooks Pro Desktop offers online chat support for immediate assistance.

- Similar to phone support, you can find the chat option on the Intuit QuickBooks website or within your software (refer to documentation for specific location).

- Online chat availability might be limited compared to phone support hours.

**Community Forum:**

- The Intuit QuickBooks website offers a community forum where you can search for solutions to common problems or post your questions for help from other QuickBooks users and professionals.

- While not a direct line to QuickBooks support, the community forum can be a valuable resource for troubleshooting and finding solutions from the user community.

**Important Considerations:**

- **Limited Free Support:** Free technical phone support for QuickBooks Pro Desktop might be limited, especially for older versions. You might encounter prompts to upgrade to a paid support plan to access extended assistance.

- **Paid Support Options:** Intuit offers paid support plans that provide priority access to phone support and potentially additional benefits like online training or data recovery assistance. Consider these options if you require ongoing technical support.

- **Version Limitations:** Free and paid support options might have limitations on the versions of QuickBooks Pro Desktop they cover. Ensure you check if your version is eligible for support before contacting them.

**Alternative Resources:**

- **QuickBooks Pro Advisor:** Consider seeking help from an Intuit Certified QuickBooks Pro Advisor. These professionals are trained on QuickBooks products and can provide personalized guidance for a fee.

- **Online Resources:** Numerous websites and online communities offer tutorials, troubleshooting guides, and other resources for QuickBooks Pro Desktop users. Explore these resources alongside contacting QuickBooks support.

By understanding the available contact options and considering the limitations, you can choose the most appropriate way to reach QuickBooks support and get the assistance you need to resolve your QuickBooks Pro Desktop issues.

## Accessing QuickBooks Community Forums

While contacting QuickBooks support directly is an option, the QuickBooks Community Forums can be a valuable resource for troubleshooting and finding solutions. Here's how to access them:

**1. Intuit QuickBooks Website:**

- The official entry point for the QuickBooks Community Forums is through the Intuit QuickBooks website.

**2. Finding the Community Section:**

- There are a couple of ways to locate the community section depending on your specific landing page:

  o **Top Navigation Bar:** Look for a tab or menu option labelled "Community" or "Support Community".

  o **Search Bar:** Utilize the search bar on the Intuit website and type "QuickBooks Community Forums" or similar keywords.

- Clicking on the Community link will take you to the dedicated community forum page.

## 3. Navigating the Forums:

- Once on the community forum page, you'll find various sections categorized by QuickBooks product (QuickBooks Online, QuickBooks Pro Desktop, etc.).

- Look for the section specific to QuickBooks Pro Desktop.

- Within the QuickBooks Pro Desktop forum section, you'll see categories or boards dedicated to different functionalities (e.g., Invoicing, Banking, Reports).

## 4. Searching and Posting:

- **Search Bar:** The forum likely has a search bar where you can type in keywords related to your issue and see if there are existing discussions or solutions.

- **Posting a New Question:** If you can't find an answer through search, you can create a new post detailing your question or problem.

- Clearly describe the issue you're facing, the steps you've already tried, and any error messages encountered. The more details you provide, the better chance you'll get helpful responses from other users or QuickBooks professionals.

## Benefits of Using the Community Forums:

- **Free Resource:** The QuickBooks Community Forums are a free resource accessible to all QuickBooks users.

- **Knowledge Sharing:** The forums offer a platform to learn from other users' experiences and solutions to common QuickBooks Pro Desktop challenges.

- **Diverse Perspectives:** You might find insights and solutions from different users with varying levels of expertise.

- **Community Support:** The forum fosters a sense of community where you can connect with other QuickBooks users and get help from experienced individuals.

## Keep in mind:

- **Response Time:** While some users and moderators might respond quickly, replies on the forum can take some time depending on the activity and complexity of your question.

- **Accuracy of Information:** It's advisable to critically evaluate the information you find on the forums. While most users strive to be helpful, some advice might not be entirely accurate. Look for responses from users with established reputations or moderators for increased reliability.

By leveraging the QuickBooks Community Forums alongside other support options, you can effectively troubleshoot issues, learn best practices, and gain valuable insights from the QuickBooks user community.

# CHAPTER TWELVE
# ADVANCED FEATURES

## Multi-Currency Support

QuickBooks Pro Desktop includes multi-currency support to help businesses manage transactions in different currencies. This feature is particularly useful for companies that deal with international clients, vendors, or transactions. Here's how to set up and use multi-currency in QuickBooks Pro Desktop:

**Enabling Multi-Currency**

1. Open QuickBooks Desktop:

   - Launch QuickBooks Pro Desktop on your computer.

2. Access Preferences:

   - Go to the Edit menu and select Preferences.

3. Select Multiple Currencies:

   - In the left pane, click on Multiple Currencies.

4. Enable Multi-Currency:

   - Click on the Company Preferences tab.

   - Select Yes, I use more than one currency.

   - Click OK to save your changes.

Note: Once multi-currency is enabled, it cannot be turned off, so ensure this feature is necessary for your business operations before activating it.

**Adding Foreign Currencies**

1. Go to Currency List:

   - Navigate to the Lists menu and select Currency List.

2. Add New Currency:

   - Click the Currency drop-down and select New.

- Choose the currency you want to add from the list.

- Click OK to add the currency to your Currency List.

**Assigning Currencies to Customers, Vendors, and Accounts**

1. Assign Currency to Customers:

    - Go to the Customer Centre.

    - Select the customer you want to assign a currency to.

    - Click Edit.

    - In the Currency field, select the appropriate currency for the customer.

    - Click OK to save the changes.

2. Assign Currency to Vendors:

    - Go to the Vendor Centre.

    - Select the vendor you want to assign a currency to.

    - Click Edit.

    - In the Currency field, select the appropriate currency for the vendor.

    - Click OK to save the changes.

3. Assign Currency to Accounts:

    - Go to the Chart of Accounts.

    - Select the account you want to assign a currency to.

    - Click Edit.

    - In the Currency field, select the appropriate currency for the account.

    - Click OK to save the changes.

**Handling Multi-Currency Transactions**

1. Creating Invoices in Foreign Currencies:

- When creating an invoice for a customer assigned a foreign currency, QuickBooks automatically uses that currency for the transaction.

- Enter the details of the invoice as usual. The amounts will be in the customer's currency.

2. Entering Bills in Foreign Currencies:

- When entering a bill for a vendor assigned a foreign currency, QuickBooks automatically uses that currency for the transaction.

- Enter the details of the bill as usual. The amounts will be in the vendor's currency.

3. Recording Foreign Currency Payments:

- Payments received or made in foreign currencies should be recorded in the respective currency.

- QuickBooks will handle the conversion based on the exchange rate at the time of the transaction.

**Managing Exchange Rates**

1. Updating Exchange Rates:

- QuickBooks allows you to update exchange rates manually.

- Go to the Lists menu and select Currency List.

- Double-click the currency you want to update.

- Enter the new exchange rate and click OK.

2. Automatic Exchange Rate Updates:

- QuickBooks can automatically update exchange rates if connected to the internet. Ensure you check for updates regularly to keep rates current.

**Reporting in Multi-Currency**

1. Running Reports:

- QuickBooks provides several reports that support multi-currency, including Profit and Loss by Currency and Balance Sheet by Currency.

- Access these reports through the Reports menu.

2. Customizing Reports:

   - Customize reports to display amounts in different currencies as needed.

   - Use the Customize Report button to adjust the currency settings.

Multi-currency support in QuickBooks Pro Desktop simplifies the management of international transactions, ensuring accuracy in financial reporting and compliance with global accounting standards.

## Job Costing and Project Management

QuickBooks Pro Desktop provides robust tools for job costing and project management, enabling businesses to track expenses and revenues for specific jobs or projects. This helps in determining the profitability of individual jobs and managing project-related finances effectively. Here's how to utilize these features:

**Setting Up Jobs**

1. **Create a Customer**:

   - Before you can set up a job, ensure that you have a customer to associate it with.

   - Go to the **Customer Centre**.

   - Click **New Customer & Job** and select **New Customer**.

   - Enter the customer details and click **OK**.

2. **Create a Job for a Customer**:

   - In the **Customer Centre**, select the customer you created.

   - Click **New Customer & Job** and select **Add Job**.

   - Enter the job name and details such as job description, start date, projected end date, and job type.

- Click **OK** to save the job.

**Tracking Job Costs**

1. **Assign Expenses to Jobs**:

   - When entering expenses, such as bills or checks, make sure to assign them to the appropriate job.

   - In the expense form, select the customer: job in the **Customer: Job** column.

2. **Record Time for Jobs**:

   - Use the **Weekly Timesheet** or **Single Activity** form to record time spent on jobs.

   - In the timesheet, select the customer: job for each time entry.

   - If you have employees or subcontractors working on the job, ensure their time is accurately recorded and associated with the correct job.

3. **Enter Invoices for Jobs**:

   - When invoicing customers for work completed, ensure the invoice is associated with the correct job.

   - Select the customer: job in the **Customer: Job** field on the invoice form.

**Managing Project Finances**

1. **Estimate Costs for Jobs**:

   - Create estimates to forecast the costs associated with a job.

   - Go to the **Customers** menu, select **Create Estimates**, and enter the details for the job.

   - This helps in comparing estimated costs with actual costs incurred.

2. **Create Progress Invoices**:

   - If you bill customers in stages, use progress invoicing.

- Convert an estimate to an invoice for a portion of the total job cost by selecting **Create Invoices** from the **Customers** menu and choosing to create an invoice based on the estimate.

3. **Track Job Expenses and Revenue**:

- Regularly review job-related expenses and revenues to ensure the job is on budget.

- Use reports such as **Job Profitability Summary** and **Job Profitability Detail** to analyse the financial performance of each job.

## Reporting for Job Costing

1. **Job Reports**:

- QuickBooks Pro Desktop offers a variety of reports to help you manage job costs and assess profitability.

- Access job reports by going to the **Reports** menu, selecting **Jobs, Time & Mileage**, and choosing from the available reports, such as:

  - **Job Profitability Summary**

  - **Job Profitability Detail**

  - **Job Estimates vs. Actuals Summary**

  - **Job Estimates vs. Actuals Detail**

2. **Customize Job Reports**:

- Customize reports to focus on specific jobs or time periods.

- Use the **Customize Report** button to filter data, add or remove columns, and adjust the report layout according to your needs.

## Using QuickBooks Projects (Optional)

1. **Enable Projects**:

- QuickBooks Pro Desktop has a Projects feature that allows for more detailed tracking and management of projects.

- To enable Projects, go to the **Customers** menu and select **Projects**.

2. **Create a Project**:

   - After enabling Projects, create a new project by selecting a customer and adding a project.

   - Enter the project name, description, start and end dates, and other relevant details.

3. **Manage Project Finances**:

   - Track project expenses, invoices, and profitability through the Projects interface.

   - Use project-specific reports to monitor progress and financial performance.

By effectively utilizing job costing and project management features in QuickBooks Pro Desktop, businesses can gain detailed insights into the financial health of their projects, ensuring better budget management and profitability tracking.

# Budgeting and Forecasting

QuickBooks Pro Desktop provides powerful tools for budgeting and forecasting, allowing businesses to plan their finances, set financial goals, and measure performance against these targets. Here's how to utilize these features:

**Creating Budgets**

1. **Access the Budgeting Tool**:

   - Go to the **Company** menu and select **Planning & Budgeting**, then choose **Set Up Budgets**.

2. **Create a New Budget**:

   - Click **Create New Budget**.

   - Select the fiscal year for the budget.

   - Choose the type of budget you want to create:

     - **Profit and Loss**: Budget by income and expense accounts.

- **Balance Sheet**: Budget by asset, liability, and equity accounts.

3. **Specify Additional Criteria**:

   - Choose whether to budget for the entire company or by customer: job.

   - For more detailed tracking, you can also create budgets by class if you use class tracking.

4. **Enter Budget Data**:

   - Manually enter your budgeted amounts for each account and each month.

   - You can also use the **Copy From Last Year** feature to use previous year's data as a starting point.

5. **Save the Budget**:

   - Once you've entered all the data, click **Save** to finalize your budget.

## Managing Budgets

1. **Review and Edit Budgets**:

   - To view or edit an existing budget, go to the **Company** menu, select **Planning & Budgeting**, and choose **Set Up Budgets**.

   - Select the budget you want to review or edit.

   - Make any necessary adjustments and save your changes.

2. **Compare Actuals to Budget**:

   - QuickBooks allows you to compare actual financial performance against your budget.

   - Use the **Budget vs. Actual** report to see variances between budgeted amounts and actual figures.

## Forecasting

1. **Access the Forecasting Tool**:

   - Go to the **Company** menu and select **Planning & Budgeting**, then choose **Set Up Forecasts**.

2. **Create a New Forecast**:

   - Click **Create New Forecast**.

   - Select the fiscal year for the forecast.

   - Choose the type of forecast you want to create (typically Profit and Loss).

3. **Enter Forecast Data**:

   - Manually enter your forecasted amounts for each account and each month.

   - You can also use the **Create From Previous Year's Actual Data** feature to generate a forecast based on past performance.

4. **Save the Forecast**:

   - Once you've entered all the data, click **Save** to finalize your forecast.

**Using Budgets and Forecasts for Financial Planning**

1. **Run Budget and Forecast Reports**:

   - QuickBooks provides several reports to help you analyse your budget and forecast data.

   - Go to the **Reports** menu, select **Budgets & Forecasts**, and choose from the available reports, such as:

     - **Budget Overview**: Summarizes your budget by account.

     - **Budget vs. Actual**: Compares actual figures to your budget.

     - **Forecast Overview**: Summarizes your forecast by account.

     - **Forecast vs. Actual**: Compares actual figures to your forecast.

2. **Customize Reports**:

   - Customize these reports to focus on specific accounts, time periods, or departments.

   - Use the **Customize Report** button to filter data, add or remove columns, and adjust the report layout according to your needs.

3. **Adjusting Budgets and Forecasts**:

   - Regularly review your budgets and forecasts to ensure they remain accurate and relevant.

   - Make adjustments as needed based on changes in business conditions or financial performance.

**Tips for Effective Budgeting and Forecasting**

- **Involve Key Stakeholders**: Engage department heads and financial managers in the budgeting and forecasting process to gather accurate data and realistic projections.

- **Use Historical Data**: Analyse past financial performance to inform your budgeting and forecasting assumptions.

- **Monitor Regularly**: Regularly compare actual performance to budgets and forecasts to identify variances and adjust plans as necessary.

- **Be Realistic**: Set achievable goals and assumptions to ensure your budgets and forecasts are practical and attainable.

By leveraging the budgeting and forecasting tools in QuickBooks Pro Desktop, businesses can effectively plan for the future, monitor financial performance, and make informed decisions to achieve their financial goals.

# Customizing Forms and Templates

QuickBooks Pro Desktop allows you to customize various forms and templates to match your business needs and branding. This includes invoices, estimates, sales receipts, and more. Here's how to customize forms and templates:

**Accessing the Form Templates**

1. **Open the Form Templates**:

   - Go to the **Lists** menu.

   - Select **Templates**.

2. **Select a Template to Customize**:

- In the Template List, choose the type of form you want to customize (e.g., Invoice, Estimate, Sales Receipt).

- Double-click on the template you want to customize or click **Templates** and select **Edit Template**.

**Customizing Templates**

1. **Use the Basic Customization Tool**:

- In the **Basic Customization** window, you can modify the overall look and feel of the template.

- **Logo**: Add or change the company logo by clicking on **Use Logo** and selecting your logo file.

- **Colour Scheme**: Change the colour scheme by selecting a predefined colour or creating a custom colour.

- **Fonts & Numbers**: Customize the fonts and number formats used in the template.

2. **Layout Designer for Advanced Customization**:

- Click **Additional Customization** for more detailed changes.

- In the **Additional Customization** window, you can modify the header, columns, footer, and print layout.

  - **Header**: Add or remove fields in the header section (e.g., company name, address, phone number).

  - **Columns**: Customize the columns displayed on the form, including adding new columns or changing their order.

  - **Footer**: Add or modify fields in the footer section (e.g., customer message, thank you note).

3. **Using the Layout Designer**:

- For precise control over the layout, click **Layout Designer**.

- In the **Layout Designer** window, you can drag and drop elements to rearrange them on the form.

  - **Add Fields**: Click **Add** and select the type of field to add (e.g., text box, data field).

  - **Move Elements**: Click and drag elements to move them to the desired location.

  - **Resize Elements**: Click on the edges of an element to resize it.

  - **Align Elements**: Use alignment tools to align elements horizontally or vertically.

4. **Preview and Save the Template**:

- Use the **Preview** button to see how the template will look when printed.

- Once satisfied with the customization, click **OK** to save the changes.

- Optionally, use **Save As** to create a new template based on your customization, allowing you to keep the original template unchanged.

**Applying Customized Templates**

1. **Set a Default Template**:

- To set a customized template as the default for a particular form type:

  - Go to **Lists > Templates**.

  - Right-click the customized template and select **Make Default**.

2. **Use a Template for a Specific Transaction**:

- When creating a transaction (e.g., invoice, estimate), you can select the template to use:

  - In the transaction window, choose the **Template** drop-down menu.

  - Select the desired template from the list.

**Customizing Other Forms**

1. **Sales Orders, Purchase Orders, and Other Forms**:

   - Follow similar steps to customize other forms such as sales orders and purchase orders.

   - Access the templates through the **Lists** menu, select the appropriate form type, and follow the customization steps outlined above.

2. **Batch Invoices and Statements**:

   - For batch invoicing or statements, customize the templates similarly to ensure consistency in branding and layout.

**Tips for Effective Customization**

- **Consistent Branding**: Ensure that your company logo, colours, and fonts are consistent across all forms to maintain a professional appearance.

- **Clear Information**: Make sure all necessary information is clearly displayed, and avoid cluttering the form with too much detail.

- **Test Printing**: Always test print your customized forms to ensure they appear as expected and adjust if necessary.

- **Save Versions**: Save different versions of templates for different purposes (e.g., a detailed invoice template and a simplified one).

By customizing forms and templates in QuickBooks Pro Desktop, you can create professional, branded documents that meet your business needs and enhance communication with your customers.

## Integrating QuickBooks with Other Applications

QuickBooks Pro Desktop offers limited built-in functionality for integrating with other applications. However, there are two main approaches to connect QuickBooks Pro Desktop with other software programs to enhance its capabilities:

**1. Third-Party Add-On Applications:**

- A wide range of third-party add-on applications integrate with QuickBooks Pro Desktop, extending its functionalities in various areas. These add-ons can connect to services like:

  - **E-commerce platforms (Shopify, WooCommerce):** Automate data flow between your online store and QuickBooks for seamless sales and inventory management.

  - **Customer Relationship Management (CRM) software (Salesforce, Zoho):** Synchronize customer data and improve communication between your sales and accounting teams.

  - **Payroll processing services (ADP, Paychex):** Streamline payroll tasks by integrating payroll data with your accounting software.

  - **Inventory management software (Zoho Inventory, Fishbowl):** Enhance inventory tracking and control beyond QuickBooks Pro Desktop's basic functionalities.

- **Benefits of Add-Ons:**

  - Increased automation and efficiency by streamlining data flow between applications.

  - Improved data accuracy by reducing manual data entry.

  - Enhanced functionalities in specific areas like inventory management, CRM, or e-commerce.

- **Considerations for Add-Ons:**

  - **Evaluation and Selection:** Carefully research and choose add-on applications that are compatible with your version of QuickBooks Pro Desktop and that meet your specific needs.

  - **Cost:** Third-party add-ons often come with additional subscription fees. Factor in the cost when evaluating the return on investment.

  - **Security and Integration:** Ensure the add-on is reputable and integrates securely with QuickBooks Pro Desktop to minimize data security risks.

  - **Support and Updates:** Choose an add-on with reliable customer support and that offers regular updates for compatibility and security.

## 2. Data Import/Export:

- While not a true integration, QuickBooks Pro Desktop allows you to import and export data in specific formats like CSV or Excel files. This enables some level of data exchange with other software programs.

- **Use Cases for Import/Export:**

  - **Migrating Data from Another System:** You can potentially import data from a previous accounting system or a spreadsheet into QuickBooks Pro Desktop.

  - **Sharing Data with Other Applications:** Export specific data sets from QuickBooks Pro Desktop for use in other software programs (e.g., exporting customer data for a marketing campaign).

- **Limitations of Import/Export:**

  - **Manual Work Required:** The import/export process often requires manual formatting and mapping of data fields, which can be time-consuming and error-prone.

  - **Limited Functionality:** Data import/export doesn't offer real-time integration or bi-directional data flow between applications.

## Choosing the Right Approach:

The best approach for integrating QuickBooks Pro Desktop with other applications depends on your specific needs and the complexity of the desired data exchange.

- **For basic data exchange or occasional needs, data import/export might suffice.**

- **For more complex data flow, automation, and enhanced functionalities, consider investing in third-party add-on applications.**

It's crucial to carefully evaluate your requirements, research available add-on options, and ensure secure and reliable integration methods to maximize the benefits of connecting QuickBooks Pro Desktop with other software programs in your business ecosystem.

# CHAPTER THIRTEEN
# APPENDIX

## Keyboard Shortcuts

QuickBooks Pro Desktop offers a variety of keyboard shortcuts to help you navigate and perform tasks more efficiently. Here are some of the most commonly used shortcuts:

**General Navigation**

- **Ctrl + N**: Create a new transaction or list item.

- **Ctrl + E**: Edit the selected transaction or list item.

- **Ctrl + D**: Delete the selected transaction or list item.

- **Ctrl + F**: Find a transaction.

- **Ctrl + J**: Open the Customer Centre.

- **Ctrl + Q**: QuickReport on the selected transaction or list item.

- **Ctrl + R**: Open the Register for the selected account.

- **Ctrl + W**: Write a new check.

- **Ctrl + I**: Create a new invoice.

- **Ctrl + M**: Memorize a transaction.

- **Ctrl + T**: Open the Memorized Transaction List.

- **Ctrl + U**: Use List Item (e.g., use a customer, vendor, or item in a transaction).

**File and Window Management**

- **Ctrl + O**: Open an existing company file.

- **Ctrl + P**: Print the current form or report.

- **Ctrl + Q**: Close QuickBooks.

- **Ctrl + G**: Go to the previous window.

- **Ctrl + Tab**: Move between open QuickBooks windows.

## Date Shortcuts

- **+**: Increase the date by one day.

- **-**: Decrease the date by one day.

- **T**: Set the date to today.

- **Y**: Set the date to the beginning of the year.

- **R**: Set the date to the end of the year.

- **M**: Set the date to the beginning of the month.

- **H**: Set the date to the end of the month.

- **W**: Set the date to the beginning of the week.

- **K**: Set the date to the end of the week.

## List Navigation

- **Ctrl + L**: Open the list (e.g., Customer List, Vendor List).

- **Ctrl + Insert**: Insert a line in a transaction list.

- **Ctrl + Delete**: Delete a line in a transaction list.

## Reports and Graphs

- **F2**: Display the Product Information window.

- **F3**: Open the Search feature.

- **F4**: Open the Accountant Centre.

- **F5**: Refresh the active window.

- **F6**: Open the QuickBooks Messenger.

- **F7**: Open the Check Detail Report.

- **F8**: Open the Transaction Journal.

- **F9**: Display the Bill Tracker.

- **F10**: Display the Item List.

- **F11**: Open the Customer Snapshot.

- **F12**: Open the Vendor Snapshot.

**Transactions**

- **Ctrl + Alt + Y**: Create a Credit Memo/Refund.

- **Ctrl + Alt + V**: Create a Vendor Credit.

These shortcuts can significantly speed up your workflow in QuickBooks Pro Desktop, allowing you to perform tasks more quickly and efficiently.

# QuickBooks Pro Desktop FAQ

Here are some frequently asked questions (FAQs) about QuickBooks Pro Desktop:

**General Features:**

- **What is QuickBooks Pro Desktop?**

QuickBooks Pro Desktop is an on-premise accounting software program designed for small and medium-sized businesses. It helps manage finances by tracking income and expenses, creating invoices and bills, generating reports, and managing inventory.

- **What are the benefits of using QuickBooks Pro Desktop?**

    o   User-friendly interface for managing finances.

    o   Wide range of features for invoicing, bill management, and reporting.

    o   Ability to manage inventory.

    o   Secure storage of financial data on your local computer (for some users, this is a benefit over cloud-based solutions).

- **What are the drawbacks of QuickBooks Pro Desktop?**

o   Requires installation and setup on each computer that needs access.

o   Manual backups are necessary to ensure data security.

o   Limited real-time collaboration compared to cloud-based solutions.

**Getting Started:**

- **How do I install QuickBooks Pro Desktop?**

You can download the installation file from the Intuit website and follow the on-screen instructions. The system requirements will vary depending on the version, so ensure your computer meets them before installation.

- **How do I set up a new company file?**

When you launch QuickBooks Pro Desktop for the first time, you'll be prompted to create a new company file. You'll need to enter your business information, set up your chart of accounts, and add information about customers and vendors.

- **What resources are available to help me learn QuickBooks Pro Desktop?**

Intuit offers a variety of resources, including video tutorials, documentation, and webinars to help you learn QuickBooks Pro Desktop. You can find these resources on the Intuit QuickBooks website.

**Data Management:**

- **Can I import data from other software programs?**

QuickBooks Pro Desktop doesn't directly support data import through code. However, you can import specific data sets from CSV or Excel files by following the software's import guidelines.

- **How do I set up users and permissions?**

QuickBooks Desktop allows you to grant access to your company file to multiple users. You can create user roles with specific permissions to control what each user can see and do within the software.

- **How do I back up my company file?**

It's crucial to regularly back up your company file to prevent data loss. QuickBooks Pro Desktop offers built-in backup functionalities. You can also explore third-party backup solutions for added security.

**Additional Questions:**

- **Where can I find information about keyboard shortcuts?**

Keyboard shortcuts can be found within the Help menu, the Chart of Accounts menu, or through online resources on the Intuit QuickBooks website.

- **How much does QuickBooks Pro Desktop cost?**

Pricing for QuickBooks Pro Desktop varies depending on the version and features you choose. You can find current pricing information on the Intuit QuickBooks website.

- **Is QuickBooks Pro Desktop right for my business?**

QuickBooks Pro Desktop is a suitable option for small and medium-sized businesses that need a comprehensive accounting solution with on-premise data storage. However, if you require real-time collaboration features or prefer a cloud-based solution, you might consider QuickBooks Online.

This list provides a starting point for your QuickBooks Pro Desktop FAQs. Remember, you can find more specific information and detailed answers to your questions through the resources provided by Intuit QuickBooks.